THE POVERTY OF CORRUPT NATIONS

ROY CULLEN

Order this book online at www.trafford.com/07-0953
or email orders@trafford.com

Most Trafford titles are also available at major online book retailers.

© Copyright 2007 Roy Cullen.
All rights reserved. No part of this publication may be reproduced, stored in a retrieval system, or transmitted, in any form or by any means, electronic, mechanical, photocopying, recording, or otherwise, without the written prior permission of the author.

Note for Librarians: A cataloguing record for this book is available from Library and Archives Canada at www.collectionscanada.ca/amicus/index-e.html

Printed in Victoria, BC, Canada.

ISBN: 978-1-4251-2775-6

We at Trafford believe that it is the responsibility of us all, as both individuals and corporations, to make choices that are environmentally and socially sound. You, in turn, are supporting this responsible conduct each time you purchase a Trafford book, or make use of our publishing services. To find out how you are helping, please visit www.trafford.com/responsiblepublishing.html

Our mission is to efficiently provide the world's finest, most comprehensive book publishing service, enabling every author to experience success. To find out how to publish your book, your way, and have it available worldwide, visit us online at www.trafford.com/10510

 www.trafford.com

North America & international
toll-free: 1 888 232 4444 (USA & Canada)
phone: 250 383 6864 ♦ fax: 250 383 6804 ♦ email: info@trafford.com

The United Kingdom & Europe
phone: +44 (0)1865 722 113 ♦ local rate: 0845 230 9601
facsimile: +44 (0)1865 722 868 ♦ email: info.uk@trafford.com

10 9 8 7 6 5 4 3

ABOUT THE AUTHOR, HON. ROY CULLEN, P.C., M.P.

Roy Cullen was elected to the House of Commons as the Member of Parliament for Etobicoke North (Toronto) in a by-election in 1996. He was re-elected in the 1997, 2000, 2004, and 2006 General Elections.

He has served as Chair of the House of Commons Standing Committee on Finance; as Parliamentary Secretary to the Minister of Finance; as Parliamentary Secretary to the Deputy Prime Minister and the Minister for Public Safety and Emergency Preparedness; as Chair of the Ontario Liberal Caucus; and as Official Opposition Critic for Natural Resources.

During his tenure as Parliamentary Secretary to the Minister of Finance he was actively involved in designing and implementing Canada's anti-money laundering regime. Since being elected Mr. Cullen has been very active with the Global Organization of Parliamentarians Against Corruption (GOPAC) in the international fight against corruption and money laundering. He has spoken out on the scourge of corruption and money laundering and has played a leadership role at a number of anti-corruption and anti-money laundering workshops and conferences.

Mr. Cullen served as an Assistant Deputy Minister in the British Columbia Ministry of Forests and as a Vice-President in the Noranda Forest Group (now Norbord).

Mr. Cullen has a B.A. in Business Administration and a Master's of Public Administration. He qualified as a Canadian Chartered Accountant in 1972. Born in 1944 in Montreal, Mr. Cullen lived overseas and in

British Columbia before settling in Toronto. Married to Ethne, he has one son, Peter.

Roy Cullen co-chairs a meeting in Mexico City of Parliamentarians from Latin America and the Caribbean, March 2/3, 2006 on the fight against corruption and money laundering.

TABLE OF CONTENTS

About the author, Hon. Roy Cullen, P.C., M.P.   3

Introduction: Why Bother About Poverty and Corruption?   **7**

1: North – South Disparities   **13**

New Paradigm Needed   13

Official Development Assistance (ODA) Trends   15

The Environment, Labour Standards and Trade Barriers   22

International Financial Markets and their Impact on the Poor   33

2: Money Laundering and the Financing of Terrorism   **42**

3: Why Corruption is Stifling the Flow of Investment Capital   **63**

The Problem of Investment   63

4: The Diseases of Bribery and Corruption   **73**

World Corruption at a Glance   97

Corruption has a supply and a demand side   105

How do we deal with the suppliers of bribes?   106

5: Good Corporate Governance and the Role of Education and Innovation   **108**

The Relevance of Good Corporate Governance   108

The Role of Education and Innovation   110

Emigration and Globalization: More people are on the Move   135

6: How Do We Move Forward? – The 20 Point Plan   **139**

7: Conclusion   **167**

APPENDIX: The Index of Public Governance   171

Acknowledgements   193

INTRODUCTION

WHY BOTHER ABOUT POVERTY AND CORRUPTION?

It is March 2006 and Nigeria's Mining Minister, Oby Ezekwesili, is in Toronto attending the annual Prospectors and Developers Association of Canada global mining conference. She has come to the conference to convince those in attendance that Nigeria is open for business – especially for mining. The country's leadership, she asserts, is cleaning up the corruption that has suffocated Nigeria for so many years. She argues that just cleaning up the government's procurement processes has resulted in savings of about US$13 billion over the past 2½ years! This amount would apparently have left the country in the form of inflated contracts benefiting senior government officials! And this is only the beginning she says. This would be bad enough if it weren't for the fact that Nigeria is one of the poorest countries in the world (ranked 199th out of 208 countries) according to the 2003 World Bank Atlas report. In addition, according to Transparency International, an independent 'think tank', Nigeria was ranked in 2005 as one of the most corrupt nations in the world, ranking 154th out of 159 countries on the Corruption Perceptions Index (where country 159 is the most corrupt). By way of contrast, Canada ranked fourteenth on this same list (i.e. the 14th least corrupt country).

So, I suspect Ms. Ezekwesili has some convincing to do. The challenge is compounded by the significant role that the natural resource sector plays in the economy of Nigeria. For example, oil & gas production contributes about 20% of Nigeria's Gross National Product (GDP), and nearly all of its foreign exchange earnings. Good luck to Ms. Ezekwesili – she will surely need some good fortune to tackle the problems facing Nigeria. The Minister of Mining is nicknamed Madame Due Process – attributes that will be essential if Nigeria is serious about cleaning up its act.

Bribery and corruption are pervasive throughout the world – probably at their worst in Africa, Asia, South America and Eastern Europe. In the context of Africa, by way of example, from estimates derived by the African Union itself, some US$148 billion a year is lost every year to corruption. Africa is also the continent with the greatest number of people living in poverty. By contrast, Africa is also a continent rich in natural resources, owning 50% of the world's gold, 98% of its chromium, 90% of the world's cobalt, 64% of its manganese and 33% of its uranium. Nigeria's anti-corruption commission recently reported that the country's past rulers stole or misused $500 billion (equal to all the western aid to Africa in four decades!).

Something is wrong with this picture! We know that there is a high degree of correlation between poverty and corruption. A country that is poor is likely to be corrupt also; and likewise a country that is corrupt is also likely to be poor. What we don't know is which is the cause and which the effect. Did the country become poor because it was corrupt or did corruption take hold because of abject poverty? We may never know the answers to these questions but it seems obvious that if we could eliminate, or at least reduce corruption, we could make a positive impact on poverty.

A recent World Bank survey on Africa claims: "The amount stolen and now held in foreign banks is equivalent to more than half of the continent's external debt".[1] While the rest of the world looks for ways to relieve African nations of their debt burdens, which in many cases is prohibitive, these funds would be more useful in paying down some of these debts.

In the late 1990's world leaders committed themselves to alleviating poverty in Africa, but there has been very little progress in meeting this objective. In fact, Africa has slipped deeper into poverty during this period.

---

[1] World Bank Survey.

To fight the war against poverty in Africa, affluent countries must not only ensure that Africans get aid, they must get to the root of the problem by arming Africans with information and support to battle corruption. Nigeria, which is rich in oil resources, has had most of its wealth confiscated by a series of military dictators. Transparency International estimates that the late dictator Sani Abacha embezzled $5 billion of public funds, leaving people of the Niger Delta, where most of the oil comes from, in abject poverty.[2] The same is true for other African nations. The Congo, which is rich in copper, cobalt, gold and diamonds, suffers extreme poverty while the late Congolese dictator Mobutu Sese Seko is alleged to have removed for personal use $5 billion from government funds. Had these countries been given a chance to operate without the cloak of corruption, money that was misdirected could have provided a better standard of living for all the people of these nations.

The World Bank has indicated that it will strive for more transparent accounting from governments who receive their funds. As well, Canada and the rest of the world could be doing more. Canada can help these impoverished nations by empowering African citizens with information to prevent and monitor corruption. Having Canadian companies operating in the developing world ensure that all transactions are completely transparent, indicating how much money they pay to a particular government, can do this. Such is the purpose of International Organizations policy of *Publish What You Pay*, which ensures that resource rich countries are not robbed of their profits. It should be mandatory for all investing companies to be a part of coalitions like these. If Africans are not aware of the facts on corruption, they cannot hold their governments accountable. By providing this information to Africans, we can empower them to move away from corruption and one step closer to eliminating poverty.

While Africa has been receiving much of the attention of the world in their struggle with poverty and corruption, they certainly are not alone. Many other countries are poor and corrupt. It is estimated, for example, that in China, corruption accounts for 15% of the country's GDP. More than 846,000 Communist Party members were punished for corruption

---

[2] Drohan, Madelaine. How we can help Africa (without spending a cent). *The Globe and Mail*. August 2005.

from 1998 to 2002 alone, and 58,000 officials have been punished in recent years at the state-owned banks in China.[3]

Why do we keep beating our heads against the wall and not coming to grips with the underlying problem? The problem is corrupt leaders who skim off the cream for themselves and their cronies and leave their citizens to struggle for survival.

What I will attempt to demonstrate in this book is that bribery and corruption may have cultural connotations and roots – but that they are morally and economically indefensible. This book places its focus on the relationship between corruption and poverty and it has two major themes.

Firstly, there is the need for world leaders to address the growing disparities between the rich and poor nations of the world. How big is this gap and what are the trends? As David Landes highlights in his book, *The Wealth & Poverty of Nations*, "The difference in income per head between the richest industrial nation, say Switzerland, and the poorest non-industrial country, Mozambique, is about 400 to 1. Two hundred and fifty years ago, this gap between richest and poorest was perhaps 5 to 1."[4] These developments are significant and not inconsequential. Without effective intervention the problem is likely to worsen as most of the projected population increase in coming years will be in the poorest countries. It is estimated that in today's world, 20,000 people perish every day from extreme poverty (some argue that the figure is 50,000 daily deaths from poverty-related causes).

Secondly, the need to deal with bribery and corruption – one of the key factors that is slowing economic opportunities and growth in the developing world; a growing activity that is getting completely out of hand.

I then argue that conventional approaches to poverty and corruption have not worked and need to be examined. We need to begin thinking and acting creatively to develop a new paradigm. Executing corrupt officials (25 officials have met this fate in China in the past 4 years for their corrupt activities) is not the answer for progressive nations with a respect for

---

[3] Geoffrey York, *The Globe and Mail*. May 28 2005.

[4] Landes, David. *The Wealth and Poverty of Nations*, (UK: Little, Brown and Company, 1998).

human rights and the rule of law.

The two themes mentioned above are closely interconnected. The poverty of the world's poor nations is significantly exacerbated through bribery and corruption. Later in the book I will describe the high degree of correlation between poverty and corruption. Not only do the problems of income distribution amongst the political elites, the working poor, and the poverty stricken become more exaggerated; but also their hope is sapped. This in turn can lead to political instability, donor fatigue and the disappearance of much needed investment capital in the affected countries. My work in Latin America, China and Russia has convinced me that the unequal distribution of income amongst citizens in various parts of the world is becoming a very significant political problem – ironically concentrated in areas where corruption is rampant. In China and Russia, for example, a very few in the coastal areas and big cities are witnessing significant improvements in their standard of living while others are being left behind. As a consequence, societies become unstable and migration patterns change as people leave their country of birth to destinations afar as economic refugees.

We know that disparities between the rich and poor nations are not a function of poverty alone. In fact, corruption is not an unknown phenomenon in the so-called developed world. We know also that there is a strong correlation between poverty and geography. As John Kenneth Galbraith put it when he was an agricultural economist: "[If] one marks off a belt a couple of thousand miles in width encircling the earth at the equator one finds within it *no* developed countries…Everywhere the standard of living is low and the span of human life is short."[5] Tropical diseases take their toll, the lack of rainfall and water in the tropical areas can be very challenging, and cold is easier to tolerate than heat. There are many underlying reasons for the wealth and income disparities. Some of these factors are not controllable, whereas corruption, with political will, can be controlled.

This book on poverty and corruption is written by a general practitioner, someone who has worked in the public and private sectors; an individual who has worked and lived in various locations around the world, and by

---

[5] Ibid.

someone who is currently an elected Member of Parliament in Canada's House of Commons. The perspective offered in the book is based on human experience, with a pragmatic approach to suggested prescriptions and public policy responses to the challenges of poverty and corruption.

CHAPTER I

NORTH – SOUTH DISPARITIES

New Paradigm Needed

The increasing disparities between rich and poor nations as well as the growing pace of globalization, are calling out for a new paradigm in international relations by the leaders of the world. Thomas Homer-Dixon, in his book *The Ingenuity Gap,* makes the point that "...in our political systems, we need great ingenuity to set up institutions that successfully manage struggles over wealth and power."[6] He goes on to say: "As ingenuity gaps widen the gulfs of wealth and power among us, we need imagination, metaphor and empathy more than ever, to help us remember each other's essential humanity."

Since 1960, the ratio of the income of the wealthiest 20 percent of nations to the poorest 20 percent has increased from 30/1 to 74/1. In Africa, 340 million people, or half the population, live on less than US $ 1 per day. Fifty-two percent of the people in Sub-Sahara Africa live on less than US$1 per day.[7] The mortality rate of children under five years of age is 140 per 1000, and life expectancy at birth is only 54 years. Only 58% of the population has access to safe water. The rate of illiteracy for people over 15 is 41%. There are only 18 mainline telephones per 1000 people in Africa, compared with 146 for the world as a whole and 567 for

---

[6] Thomas Homer-Dixon, *The Ingenuity Gap* (New York: Alfred A. Knopf, 2000).

[7] United Nations Economic Commission for Africa, Transforming Africa's Economy: Economic Report on Africa 2000, 2001.

high-income countries.[8] It has been said that there are more telephones in Manhattan than in the entire continent of Africa, and more foreign direct investment in any one year in Singapore than there is in the continent of Africa.

It is true that poverty levels were significantly reduced in counties like China and India in the 1990's and early 2000's, but many countries continue to be left behind – especially in Africa.

"Poverty", Mahatma Gandhi once said, "is the worst form of violence."

Why should those of us in the developed world be concerned? Well, first of all our sense of what is right and wrong should start ringing a few bells. The huge disparities between the rich and the poor should cause us to reflect on whether or not this is fair and just.

There are more pragmatic reasons as well. Firstly, if we don't help the poor to help themselves, this disparity will foster discontent and instability in the world. Those who are impoverished, and believe that they are oppressed, will eventually take by force what they feel is their fair share.

As Lt. Gen. Roméo Dallaire so aptly put it in his book, *Shake Hands With the Devil*, following his experience in Rwanda: "If September 11 taught us that we have to fight and win the 'war on terrorism', it should also have taught us that if we do not immediately address the underlying (even if misguided) causes of those young terrorists' rage, we will not win the war. For every al-Qaeda bomber that we kill there will be a thousand more volunteers from all over the earth to take his place."[9] He continued by saying: "Human beings who have no rights, no security, no future, no hope and no means to survive are a desperate group who will do desperate things to take what they believe they need and deserve."

Today we are witnessing increasing levels of emigration – people taking extraordinary risks to leave the country of their birth in the hopes of achieving economic salvation. They become refugees, or more accurately economic refugees; not refugees from tyranny in the true sense. They take

---

[8] The New Partnership for Africa's Development (NEPAD), October 2001; Republic of South Africa, Department of Foreign Affairs, *Current Issues and Events*, Last Update October 29, 2001.

[9] Lgen Roméo Dallaire. *Shake Hands with the Devil* (Random House Canada, 2003).

their lives in their hands when they board a 'rust bucket' vessel and head off to a Promised Land. If economic prospects were better in the country of their birth, they would be inclined to stay there and avoid the upheaval of settlement and integration in a foreign land.

There are other reasons why the developed world should help poor countries to help themselves. More and more people are convinced that this assistance should emphasize providing developing nations with the tools they need to help themselves (i.e. provide them with fishing rods, not fish). Thomas Homer-Dixon suggests that: "Cropland and water scarcities are unquestionably limiting food output in many parts of Asia, Africa and Latin America."[10] He goes on to develop the point that a great deal more social and technical creativity in these countries would reduce many of these scarcities. Research also suggests that where per capita GDP grows, the incomes of the poor also grow – in fact typically on a one-for-one basis.

As US Secretary of State Colin Powell stated: "We have to go after poverty. We have to go after despair. We have to go after hopelessness."[11] But hopelessness cannot be tackled without first addressing the large-scale corruption in poverty-stricken nations.

Official Development Assistance (ODA) Trends

There are many challenges with international assistance. How do you identify the priority needs of the developing country? Shall we provide them with goods and services, or with the means to provide for themselves? Should we tie aid to suppliers from the country supplying the aid? Will the aid get through to the intended recipient? How effective is the aid in reducing poverty?

Assistance from the developed world to developing nations has been shrinking in the last few decades. This assistance is currently at a level of some US$52 billion, which sounds like a large sum, but it needs to be related to levels of Gross National Product (GNP). Another perspective is to relate it to other benchmarks like the level of agricultural subsidies worldwide and funds expended annually throughout the world on defence

---

[10] Thomas Homer-Dixon, *The Ingenuity Gap* (New York: Alfred A. Knopf, 2000).
[11] John C. Polanyi, *The Toronto Star,* June 16 2003.

spending. In 2002, agricultural subsidies totalled some US$311 billion, or were approximately six times total ODA. Some US$90 billion was spent on military equipment and operations – or nearly twice that spent on foreign aid.

At the Millennium Summit in September 2000 in Monterrey, Mexico, world leaders adopted specific and quantifiable development goals. Subsequently, the United Nations published 8 Millennium Development Goals in the September 6, 2001 Report of the UN Secretary General on the road map for implementation of the UN Millennium Declaration.

The 8 goals are:
- To halve, between 1990 and 2015, the proportion of people living on less than US$1 a day; and to halve, between 1990 and 2015, the proportion of people suffering from hunger;
- To ensure that, by 2015, all children can complete primary schooling;
- To eliminate gender disparity in primary and secondary education, preferably by 2005, and at all education levels no later than 2015;
- To reduce by two-thirds, between 1990 and 2015, the mortality rate for children under 5 years old;
- To reduce by three-quarters, between 1990 and 2015, the maternal mortality ratio;
- To have halted and begun to reverse by 2015 the spread of HIV/AIDS; and to have halted and begun to reverse by 2015 the incidence of malaria and other major diseases;
- To integrate the principles of sustainable development into country policies and programs and to reverse the loss of environmental resources; and to halve by 2015 the proportion of people without sustainable access to safe drinking water; and
- To develop a global partnership for development including through trade openness and debt relief.

These are ambitious goals! It has been argued by some that they are unrealistic and not attainable. Personally, I do not believe that these targets, however noble and ambitious, can be achieved and I believe it is wrong to commit to goals that cannot be reached. I hold the same view about the commitments Canada and other countries have made with respect to the Kyoto greenhouse gas emission reduction targets. While I am convinced of the need to aggressively reduce, on a global basis, the amount of greenhouse gases we emit, I don't subscribe to the idea of promising to do something that can't be done. Greenhouse gases are affecting climate change and I believe are behind the increase in natural disasters like hurricanes and flooding.

Something I learned very early in my management career was that organizational goals and objectives must be realistic and achievable. To do otherwise is to threaten one's credibility and limit the 'buy-in' of those who will have the responsibility to attain these goals. With respect to greenhouse gas reductions, it is discouraging to me that as a society we don't do more to reduce the impact of municipal solid waste on our atmosphere. Instead of pouring garbage into landfills we should be collecting the methane gas produced by rotting garbage and converting it into electricity. Escaping methane gas is far more detrimental to our ozone layer than CO^2 gases but we continue to ignore this. An aggressive plan to eliminate garbage landfills might cause us to reach our Kyoto targets. Without such a plan, however, we are doomed to fail.

My point is with respect to poverty reduction or greenhouse gas reduction targets, elected officials should avoid the temptation to generate photo opportunities to announce goals and objectives that are not attainable.[12]

The United Nations has set a target of 0.7% of Gross Domestic Product (GDP) as the target for overseas development assistance that should be allocated annually by developed countries. On a global basis,

---

[12] Gary Duncan, *The Times,* July 10 2004.

we currently are at 0.29% of GDP[13]. In Canada, for example, Overseas Development Assistance (ODA) has been cut in real terms by more that 34% since 1991/92 when it peaked at 0.49% of GDP. More recently, countries like Canada have committed to higher levels of assistance, but there is some serious catching-up to do. In the 2002 Speech from the Throne, the Government of Canada committed to doubling its Overseas Development Assistance by the year 2010. For Canada to reach the 0.7% of GDP target by 2015, additional spending of some $41 billion would be required. This is a large sum for a country like Canada and therefore the United Nations target will not soon be reached.

It is argued by Canada's Coalition to End Global Poverty that Canada, like the UK, USA, Sweden, Switzerland, Denmark, Belgium, Italy, Luxembourg, Greece and Austria, amongst others, should enact legislation to govern Overseas Development Assistance. Others, like the Aid Effectiveness Discussion Forum contend that the Government of Canada should reverse the trend of funding the vast majority (currently 70%) of CIDA's budget through multilateral agencies and foreign governments and increase its bilateral portfolio to at least 50% of its budget. While I am not so convinced that we should legislate our approach to ODA, I support the move to more direct funding by CIDA. Too often, funding through multilateral agencies is employed as a crutch in response to concerns about the aid getting directly to the individuals who are most in need, and not wasted or siphoned off by corrupt officials. Ironically, we lose control of our own programs and have to rely on the good work of these agencies. Canada could have more targeted impact if we carefully chose solid bilateral efforts.

Development assistance can take a number of different forms. The Heavily Indebted Poor Countries (HIPC) debt relief program was initiated by the G8 in 1996 and is administered by the IMF and the World Bank.

By way of information, the G8 is an informal group of eight countries: Canada, France, Germany, Italy, Japan, Russia, the United Kingdom and the United States of America. The European Union also participates and

---

[13] "Statistical Report of Official Development Assistance Fiscal Year 2002-2003" *Canadian International Development Agency*, Government of Canada, May 1 2004. http://www.acdi-cida.gc.ca/INET/IMAGES.NSF/vLUImages/stats/$file/StatRep_02_03.pdf>

is represented by the President of the European Commission and by the leader of the country that holds the presidency of the European Council at the time of the G8 Summit. The first Summit, with six countries participating, took place because of concerns over the economic problems that faced the world in the 1970s. It was held in 1975 in Rambouillet, France. Since then, the group has grown to eight countries, and the process has evolved from a forum dealing essentially with macroeconomic issues to an annual meeting with a broad-based agenda that addresses a wide range of international economic, political, and social issues.

The HIPC program aims to reduce the external debt of the world's poorest, most heavily indebted countries to sustainable levels. It provides substantial debt relief to these countries that undertake to implement critical social and economic reforms and use the benefits of debt relief to reduce poverty. To date, US$51.1 billion (number in reference to "HIPC Initiative: changes and estimates of Potential Costs by Creditor Group")[14] has been dealt with in this manner, with Canada's then Finance Minister, Paul Martin, leading the way.

Much more still needs to be done to provide debt relief to poor countries. Members of Parliament from Zambia, who were visiting Canada in 2003, pointed out that their country was still very heavily burdened with paying down their debt with fully 5.4% of its GDP in 2004 devoted to servicing these debts. This is a decade after plans were set in motion to cut the debt burdens of more than forty heavily indebted poor countries. "Paying for debt will absorb 7.4% of the entire market output of Malawi and a fifth of the output of the tiny state of São Tome."[15]

"Where finances are being redeployed to anti-poverty programs, as in Mozambique, rapid progress is being made in the numbers of children having regular primary education. The proportion of people living on less than US$1 a day has fallen from about two thirds to about half."

The Irish rock star, Bono, has put his public persona behind the HIPC and poverty reduction initiatives. In fact, at the 2003 Federal Liberal Party Leadership Convention in Toronto, Bono appeared as a keynote

---

[14] "Heavily Indebted Poor Countries (HIPC) Initiative Statistical Update March 31 2004", *International Monetary Fund,* May 5 2004. http://www.imf.org/external/np/hipc/2004/033104.pdf>

[15] Graham Searjeant, *The Times,* July 10 2004.

speaker at Paul Martin's rally. It is no coincidence that Bono's residence just outside of Dublin, Ireland is across the lane from the residence of Canada's Ambassador to Ireland. Ron Irwin, a former colleague of mine in the House of Commons in Ottawa and former Minister of Indian and Northern Affairs, served as Canada's Ambassador to Ireland in the late 1990's. While visiting Ireland during that period, Ron told us that when Bono was in town they would frequently get together – sometimes simply by walking outside their respective residences. I'm sure that Bono partly cultivated his relationship with Canada and Paul Martin through these exchanges.

The North-South Institute, in its brief to the House of Commons Standing Committee of Finance in 2002, argued that the debt burden of HIPC countries should be reduced by a further 30%. In their judgement, the architects of HIPC set the level of debt sustainability too high in a context of falling commodity prices and international recession. The status of commodity prices is different today so the conclusion might be different given their strong performance – and the same applies to the risk of worldwide recession. However, the need to more aggressively reduce the debt of poor governments who are committed to good governance is clear.

It was reported that in Somalia, during the civil war in the late 1980's/early 1990's, the warlord Mohamed Farrah Aidid, leader of Habr Gidr, a powerful Somalia sub clan, blocked aid to millions of Somalis and contributed to the starvation of many. This phenomenon has been repeated in many countries, many times.

Ryszard Kapuscinski, in his book, *The Shadow of the Sun*, describes the typical African warlord this way:"The warlord – he is a former officer, an ex-minister or party functionary, or some other strong individual desiring power and money, ruthless and without scruples - who, taking advantage of the disintegration of the state (to which he contributed and continues to contribute), wants to carve out for himself his own informal ministate, over which he can hold dictatorial sway. Most often, a warlord uses to this end the clan or tribe to which he belongs. Warlords are the sowers of tribal and racial hatred in Africa."[16]

He goes on to say: "When we hear that an African country is beginning to totter, we can be certain that warlords will soon appear on the scene. They are everywhere and control everything – in Angola, in Sudan, in Somalia, in Chad. What does a warlord do? Theoretically he fights with other warlords. Most frequently, however, he is busy robbing his own country's unarmed population. The warlord is the opposite of Robin Hood. He takes from the poor to enrich himself and feed his gangs. We are in a world in which misery condemns some to death and transforms others into monsters. The former are the victims, the latter are the executioners. There is no one else." He concludes: "Whoever has weapons has food. Whoever has food, has power."

The effectiveness of international aid is a vexing question. Former World Bank President, James Wolfensohn, has claimed "We're in the poverty reduction business." Some years ago, as members of a sub-committee of the House of Commons Standing Committee on Finance studying the effectiveness of aid through multilateral organizations such as the World Bank and the Inter-American Development Bank[17], I traveled to Washington, D.C. looking for answers. We met with many individuals and organizations, but one particular meeting stuck out in my mind. Robert McNamara, after serving as Secretary of Defence under President Kennedy and President Johnson from 1961-1968 [18] was President of the World Bank from 1968 to 1981. While he was emphatic on the criteria that should be used to evaluate the effectiveness of development aid – the reduction of poverty – he struggled with the related question of how to best measure this. He talked of the challenges of doing this because of measurement problems, but, more importantly, the difficulty of isolating other variables such as political upheaval, conflict, weather and its impact on crops, that might occur at the same time as the aid is being supplied. How can one say definitively that a reduction in poverty is the result of development assistance or other factors, such as bumper crop years or a more positive political climate? If someone like Robert McNamara, who

---

[16] Ryszard Kapuscinski, *The Shadow of the Sun* (New York: Knopf Canada, 2001).

[17] *Inter-American Development Bank,* April 20 2004. <http://www.iadb.org/>.

[18] "Secretaries of Defence Histories", *United States Department of Defence* April 23 2004. <http://www.defenselink.mil/specials/secdef_histories/bios/mcnamara.htm>.

headed the World Bank for thirteen years, was unable to answer these questions, evaluating the impact of development aid is surely an elusive pastime.

However difficult it is to measure progress in the alleviation of poverty, we must continue with this fight. Not to do this would be unconscionable. We need an equal determination, nonetheless, to constantly challenge the way we try to assist those who are in a state of poverty. The systems in place and the practices currently employed are not working very well and need to be fixed. Thinking 'outside the box' is not a concept that should be limited to the private sector – it is equally applicable in the area of public policy and programs. My contention is that we need to be doing this in the area of development assistance if we are truly to break the poverty cycle in the underdeveloped world. That is what this work is all about.

The Environment, Labour Standards and Trade Barriers

A great intellectual debate has raged in recent years over what is referred to as north/south issues. It is actually more than an intellectual debate – it has very serious practical ramifications for developing countries. In this parlance, north represents the predominately developed countries of the northern hemisphere, and south as the struggling countries of the south. The areas most frequently discussed are focused on environmental standards, labour standards and barriers to trade.

Environment

Is it fair, it is asked, for developing countries to face the same environmental and labour standards as developed countries? How can the developing world bear the cost of a higher hurdle of environmental performance at this stage of their growth cycle? Developed countries had the benefit of a lower bar as they developed and grew their economies. Now environmental standards have stiffened, but developing countries are at an earlier stage of development. Tougher controls on effluents, smoke stack emissions impose a cost on struggling companies. Should these rules be relaxed for developing countries until their industries reach the maturity of those in the developed world? Since most agree that strong economic performance is the best route to encourage investments in improving environmental performance, it is argued, those economies, with the passage of time, will be better positioned to make these investments if they are given more unfettered opportunities to grow in the short to medium term.

This argument is behind the agreement at Kyoto (less enthusiastically supported by the USA) to give some manoeuvring room to developing countries as they attempt to reduce greenhouse gases. I also believe that it is true that sound environmental policies inhibit the potential for corruption. There is a strong relationship between the environment in the developing world and corruption. It appears that whenever development planning in the environmental area fails to meet both the needs of the local and global communities at stake, corruption often follows: desperately poor people are forced to deforest land, poach, or go to other lengths of environmental destruction and corruption in order to survive. A good example of this is the oil crisis in Nigeria, which involves the native Ogoni people. The level of corruption that has ensued since this oil has been discovered is huge. Not only have the Ogoni people been displaced and nearly eradicated in the process of this quest for oil, but they have also not received any compensation from the oil revenues. Ken Saro-Wiwa has written extensively on this matter, and has been an Ogoni activist for years against the Nigerian administration (that time led by the dictator, Ibrahim Babangida). The book written by Ken Saro-Wiwa, *A Month and a Day: A Detention Diary,* is an excellent chronicle of his last years, leading up to his death sentence in 1994.

When looking at the relationship between poverty and the environment or poverty and corruption, the theory adopted by most international institutions has been that the two are directly linked to each other and cause a downward spiral, i.e. before we look at alleviating the destruction of the environment or the corrupt, illegal actions taken by people living in the third world, we must focus on alleviating poverty first. People in these situations are faced with little choice in the decisions they have to make inn order to survive. However, there is a report which challenges this notion: *Poverty and Environment: Priorities for Research and Policy,* prepared for the United Nations Development Program, by Tim Forsyth and Melissa Leach, Published by the Institute of Development Studies,

Sussex UK, 1998. While this report focuses solely on the environment, it does advance a new way of thinking about poverty and development - one that puts an emphasis on to the local rather than the universal experience of poverty. For instance, it looks at the use of community-based solutions to poverty as apposed to solutions rendered by governmental institutions which often restrict indigenous freedoms, or in some cases fail to immediately relieve the conditions of poverty in local communities.

Corruption in the environmental sector is distinct from any other forms because of its link to large sums of formal and informal revenues that are derived from natural products. This is especially true in developing countries that are rich in natural resources and whose economies are largely based on resource extraction. Nations such as Indonesia, Nigeria, Sierra Leone, and Colombia are highly dependent upon natural resources and are countries that Transparency International 2000 describes as losing billions to natural resource related corruption.

The cause of environmental related corruption is two-fold, on the one hand natural resources have a higher value in the black market and allow public officials to make profits from illegally issuing access to these resources, such as issuing false permits to overlook illicit consignments of endangered wildlife species. The second factor is rooted in the poor funding and weak environmental policies of the resource-rich countries. Without sufficient conservation programs or institutions in place, there is little environmental management or control. Literature on corruption in the environmental sector cites high correlations between environmental destruction and corrupt nations. According to the 2001 Environmental Sustainability Index, there is a high correlation between the level of corruption and environmental outcomes: the higher the level of corruption in a country, the lower the level of environmental sustainability.

The link between the environment and corruption is best illustrated in the environmental disasters of Mexico. The former President of Mexico, Vincente Fox, described in his speech at the National Accord for Transparency and Combating Corruption in 2001 how corruption thrives in the environmental sector because of private interests that have dominated the administration. These have granted forest, fishing and hunting permits on a discretionary basis in favour of companies that recklessly exploit Mexico's natural resources. This results in environmental inspections that allow illegal poaching, logging, and discharges in return for bribery and nepotism. These corrupted actions are fuelled by both the lack of accountability required from government officials, and the low salaries paid to officials, which entices inspectors and wardens to allow private groups to take resources illegally for bribes. This has produced environmental policy failure in Mexico and the depletion of essential resources, such as lumber; Mexico now has the third largest deforestation rate in the world.

Corruption in Mexico's enforcement has been increasing. In 1996 it was estimated that 70 to 80 percent of the judicial police were corrupt.[19] This widespread corruption has led Mexican citizens to loose faith in their government. Mexican citizens have been forced to tolerate corrupt government officials. This has fostered little respect for the rule of law, and forced them to turn to other means of governing. Such is the case of the corruption laden Mexican police force that has allowed a $7 billion a year drug trade market to flourish. This lack of legitimacy among the police in the country has led the military to take on the task of controlling the drug trade, with one-third of the military's budget being devoted to the anti-drug effort and 25, 000 Mexican soldiers involved in drug control operations. The enormous profits from drug trafficking provide the means to buy political protections, as cocaine traffickers spend as much as $500 million a year on bribery (which is more than double the budget of the Mexican attorney general's office.) The report by Mexico's Interior Ministry estimated that by 1995 there would be approximately 900 armed criminal bands in the country with 50% comprised of current or former police officers.

Mexico has responded to the drug corruption scandals by firing or transferring individual officers, or disbanding entire agencies and creating new ones. However, this has done little to solve the problem, as many fired police officers were rehired in other regions of the country and hundreds more reinstated after challenging their dismissals in court.

---

[19] Dresser, Denise. "Mexico: From PRI Predominance to Divided Democracy." Jorge I. Dominguez and Michael Shifter ed. *Constructing Democratic Governance in Latin America, Second Edition.* (Baltimore: John Hopkins University Press, 2003).

Corruption in the environmental sector has also plagued Russia. The World Wildlife Fund (WWF) estimates the Russia loses over US$1 billion due to illegal forest harvesting, processing and trade. As a result of the corruption in forest practices, the country suffers from great loss in biodiversity and has lost almost all its valuable forests which have caused major changes in the microclimate. To address this, WWF implemented the Russian Forest Program in 1994 which initiated a monitoring organization of illegal deforestation, and which has found more than twenty-four cases of illegal logging. In 2002, WWF commissioned a study by the Department of Natural Resources of Primorskiy Krai, which revealed that illegal logging in Primorskiy Krai constituted from 30 to 50 percent of the total amount of harvested timber that was exported every year. The study concluded that there were insufficient enforcement measures to fight forest crime and in order to combat corruption in the natural resource sector, legislation and policies that clearly stipulate environmental control need to be enforced. As well as having an effective monitoring system, the country must also utilize public, private and civil input in order to create a system of incentives and sanctions to reward compliance with policies. Simply banning corruption in the developing world is not enough to deter people from gaining access to the black market.

Labour Standards

Raising the level of labour standards in developing countries is a contentious issue, as it is feared that it may cause immediate economic harm to the developing countries by eliminating their competitive advantage of having cheap labour. Findings of researchers and social scientists indicate that allowing appalling working conditions to occur in the developing world will create a race to the bottom in the deterioration of labour standards. An example that illustrates the race to the bottom for poor labour standards is the competition between China and Mexico for the North American apparel market. Despite the outstanding employment growth in these sectors, apparel workers in these countries have experienced very limited wage growth, and the conditions in which they work are barely liveable.

Some make the same argument for labour standards that is made for environmental standards – i.e. is it fair for developing countries to face the labour standards as developed countries? How can the developing world bear the cost of a higher hurdle of tougher labour standards at this stage of their growth cycle? Developed countries had the benefit of a lower bar as they developed and grew their economies. Should these rules be relaxed for developing countries until their industries reach the maturity of those in the developed world? Why should minimum wages, the abolition of child labour, and other labour standards apply to developing countries? Won't applying the more rigorous standards of the developed world translate into fewer jobs in developing countries and/or a diminishment of their competitiveness? How can foreign companies operating in the 'developed world' justify their 'sweat shops' in 'third world' countries?

While I know that many or most trade unions do not support relaxing any of these rules, I am reminded of the scores of black Africans in South Africa, admittedly during the repressive apartheid era, who worked for very low wages. Higher wages would certainly have reduced their numbers. During this same period Africans from countries to the north flocked in great numbers to Johannesburg – the 'city of gold'. The same can be said about the use of child labour in countries around the world. What realistic other options do they have? Their cheap labour is surely the source of their products' comparative advantage in world markets.

What is needed, perhaps, is a South-South agreement, between countries of the developing world that would ensure governments, trade unions and workers of the developing world regulate the minimum labour standards through a social clause.[20] Southern countries as a bloc could negotiate with the North to set a minimum living wage in accordance with each country's own standard of living. Authors Chan and Ross (2003) describe this agreement as the solution to prevent further deterioration of labour standards in the South. They argue that if we allow labour standards to remain static in the developing world, we risk the possibility of more employees being unable to reap the benefits of their work, because their governments insist on having the believed competitive advantage of cheap labour. Many studies, including one by Lawrence (1995), finds that the gap between wage disparities has widened over the past 20 years, as

---

[20] Anita Chan and Robert J S Ross, "Racing to the bottom: International Trade without a Social Clause," *Third World Quarterly* 24 (6). 1011-1028 (2003): 1011.

well as a significant increase in poorly paid jobs.[21]

One way of ensuring higher standards of labour for the South is to link trade with labour standards, which would set a minimum wage, limitation of work hours, as well as occupational health and safety regulations. Canada did this when the Liberal government came to power in 1993 on the promise to renegotiate the North American Free Trade Agreement (NAFTA) that had been agreed to by the Conservative Government during their 1988-1993 mandate. Rather that a new a agreement, the North American Agreements on Labour and Environmental Cooperation were negotiated and implemented in parallel to the NAFTA. These agreements were designed to facilitate greater co-operation between the partner countries in those areas and to promote the effective enforcement of each country's laws and regulations. The idea was that improved working standards and environmental standards would go hand-in-hand with more trade amongst Canada, the U.S.A. and Mexico.

The jury is still out as to whether these labour standard and environmental standards objectives have been met, but the results have not been earth-shattering. In an article by Janine Jackson for FAIR (Fairness & Accuracy in Reporting) she had this to say: "1997 marks three years since NAFTA took effect, and, by any standard, the results are decidedly less rosy than proponents predicted. Many of the critics' concerns for workers' wages and rights - on both sides of the border – and for environmental protections are now verifiable."[22]

While many authors note the opposition from Southern countries to this initiative, (most notably from the All China Federation of Trade Unions (ACFTU), who reject two core labour standards: freedom of association and the right to collective bargaining), there are other Asian trade unions such as the Korean Confederation of Trade Unions (KCTU) and the Malaysian Trade Union Congress who support having labour standards and trade linked, although they are against the inclusion of a minimum wage. This has resulted in an alliance between Western bankers, multinationals,

---

[21] Lawrence, Robert Z. "Trade Multinationals and Labor." Working Paper 4836, *National Bureau of Economic Research*. August 1994.

[22] September/October, 1997. (FAIR –Fairness & Accuracy in Reporting) *Broken Promises* by Janine Jackson.

employers and Southern governments in favour of unrestricted trade without labour conditionality. This leaves Western labour NGOs, human rights groups and trade unions in opposition. However the opposition to higher standards of labour in the developing world is usually based on the belief that there will be a massive job loss that will accompany regulated labour standards, because of the competitive advantage lower standards of labour have in the South over the North. Thus it is not surprising that proposals made for upgrading labour standards are not welcomed by developing countries.[23]

To determine whether or not labour standards have an impact on the competitiveness of various countries, Professor Andre Raynauld of the University of Montreal (1998) conducted an analysis to determine the effects of the labour standards on the economy. In his analysis Raynauld divided countries into two groups: high and low standard countries. This division was based on the United Nations human-development index, with the top 20 countries of the index defined as the "high-standard" countries while the rest were characterized as the "low standard" countries. A statistical analysis was then conducted to determine whether high-standard countries suffered as a result of the more stringent labour standards they applied. The findings were that between 1970 and 1993 none of the 20 countries with 'high-standards' had experienced any drop in export market share. Among the 145 low-standards countries, only 23 (16 percent) had their export share increase over that period. Raynauld's findings indicate that labour standards have had no significant negative impact on the competitiveness of the developed countries, which is also the conclusion reached by the OECD's 1994 Employment Outlook Study,[24] that also found no correlation between labour standards and overall trade performance.

With regard to foreign direct investment inflows, Raynauld used the same index to calculate FDI inflows, and found that labour standards did not have any major negative impact on high standard of living countries.

---

[23] Raynauld, Andre. *Labour Standards and International Competitiveness: A Comparative Analysis of Developing and Industrialized Countries.* (Cheltenham, UK: Edward Elgar Publishing,1998).

[24] Organization for Economic Co-operation and Development. *OECD Employment Outlook,* July 1994. Paris, Chapter 4, Labour Standards and Economic Integration.

Despite the notion that high labour standards would result in FDI being relocated to low standard regions, only two of the low standard countries saw their share increase. Further, findings from Raynauld's study reveal countries with low wages as a result of low labour standards, also have significantly lower productivity. This suggests that it may also be in the interest of investors to pursue higher labour standards, in order to yield more productivity.

According to these findings, adopting higher labour standards is not only a matter of human rights - as a living wage to provide a decent standard of living should be a norm that is enjoyed in every social setting, regardless of whether one lives in the North or the South. Adopting higher labour standards is also a benefit to all of society as the health and occupational safety benefits enjoyed by workers will produce greater productivity and as a result, may promote higher educational achievement which is valuable to the whole of the country.

Notwithstanding these sound arguments, my own view is that the developed world should encourage in an evolutionary way, rather than a revolutionary way, improvements in environmental and labour standards in developing countries. Jeffrey Sachs is an acknowledged world expert on poverty reduction. He is Special Advisor to United Nations Secretary-General Kofi Annan on the Millennium Development Goals, and has spent twenty-five years advising governments and NGO's on poverty reduction strategies. In his book, *The End of Poverty*[25], he describes the extreme poverty in Bangladesh and how many Bangladeshi women in Dhaka, the capital of Bangladesh, have lifted themselves out of poverty, and made themselves more independent, by working long hours for low wages in the garment factories. These 'sweatshop' jobs are a target for public protesters around the globe – but the women who work there, while acknowledging the arduous conditions and poor pay, see these jobs as the first step out of extreme poverty. When Jeffrey Sachs interviewed these workers they asserted that these garment factory jobs were "the greatest opportunity that these women could ever have imagined, and that their employment had changed their lives for the better"[26]. Sachs goes on to

---

[25] Jeffrey D. Sachs, *The End of Poverty,* (New York: The Penguin Press, 2005).
[26] Ibid.

say, "Some rich-country protesters have argued that Dhaka's apparel firms should either pay far higher wage rates or be closed, but closing such factories as a result of wages forced above worker productivity would be little more than a ticket for these women back to rural misery. For these young women, these factories offer not only opportunities for personal freedom, but also the first rung on the ladder of rising skills and income for themselves and within a few years, for their children. Virtually every poor country that has developed successfully has gone through these first stages of industrialization."[27]

In our zeal to help workers who receive substandard pay (by western standards), or attempt to raise the bar of environmental performance too quickly, we may inadvertently push people back into poverty. While focussing attention on these issues can have positive affects, we should not, in my view, be arbitrary and prescriptive in the responses we propose. Better labour and environmental standards which are harmonized with the developed world as a quid pro quo for international recognition, however well intentioned, will act against their best interests. We need to keep the pressure on countries in the developing world to improve their labour and environmental standards over time – with realistic goals and a timetable that is reasonable and pragmatic.

Trade Barriers

This brings us to tariff and non-tariff trade barriers – those that diminish the ability of developing countries to sell their products and services into Europe and North America. These constraints mean that developing countries are unable to reap the benefit of this economic activity – jobs and prosperity. Developing countries who have achieved the greatest success in alleviating poverty are the same countries whose economies have grown through trade.

We need to extend duty-free and quota-free access to the economies of developed countries from the Least Developed Countries (referred to as LCD's) and identified by the UN as the 49 poorest countries in the world. For countries like Canada, this should also include supply-managed agricultural products (dairy, poultry and eggs).

---

[27] Ibid.

In 2001 the World Trade Organization (WTO) launched a broad round of talks in Qatar to lower global trade barriers. The Doha round, as it has come to be known as, called on the industrialized world to provide lower cost access to patented medicines and to reduce or eliminate distorting agricultural subsidies. The Doha round of trade talks has now collapsed, with the result that many countries are now more aggressively pursuing bilateral arrangements. This development is very unfortunate, because developing countries need cheap drugs if they have any hope of combating serious disease and illness in their countries, including the scourge of HIV/AIDS. Huge agricultural subsidies in Europe and the United States distort the international agricultural markets and create an uneven playing field between industrial countries and developing countries.

So, what does all this mean? Well it means a number of things. It means that there are many reasons why some nations are poor. It also means that we need to deal more effectively with world poverty – and there are many ways of doing this. We need to start thinking 'outside the box' to find new solutions and approaches. We need to 'rev up' the levels of overseas development assistance from the more developed economies of the world. We need to remove trade barriers to give greater assess to world markets for the products of the least developed countries. We need to think very pragmatically about the issues that surround labour and environmental standards. But the part we need to really focus in on, in my judgement, is corruption. To do otherwise is to miss one of the key, if not the most important impediment in the fight against world poverty.

Only ten years ago, the word 'corruption' was not in the vocabulary of the World Bank. "Its staff spoke instead of 'implicit taxes' or 'rent-seeking behaviour' lest they be accused of meddling in politics."[28] Fortunately, James Wolfensohn, when he became President of the World Bank, decided that corruption had to come out of the closet and be dealt with. Political correctness, he decided, had to take a back seat to economy, efficiency and justice. We must thank Mr. Wolfensohn for taking this stance – which at the time, and in that context, was very courageous.

I find it to be amazing that in the scholarly work by Jeffrey Sachs in

---

[28] *The Economist*, March 4th-10th 2005.

his 2005 book, *The End of Poverty*[29], one cannot locate a reference to the word corruption in the book index! Jeffrey Sachs is considered to be a world leading thinker in the fight against poverty. In fairness to Mr. Sachs, his book contains a chapter entitled, *Myths and Magic Bullets*, where three pages are devoted to corruption - under the heading *Corruption is the Culprit*. Three pages devoted to corruption in a book of 368 pages! In this part of his book he argues that in Africa corruption is used as an excuse not to fight poverty on that continent. He then argues that "Africa's governance is poor because Africa is poor."[30] In saying this he makes the classical mistake of drawing a conclusion as to cause and effect between poverty and corruption and their correlation. I will demonstrate later that there is a clear correlation between the level of corruption in a country, and its income per capita. What is not known is which comes first; are countries poor because they are corrupt or are they corrupt because they are poor? No one knows this – not even Mr. Sachs. I have come to the conclusion that since we will never know what the causal relationship is between poverty and corruption, we need to tackle both. We cannot, in my judgement, allow ourselves the luxury of avoiding dealing with corruption – the stakes are just too high.

International Financial Markets and their Impact on the Poor

The mid 1990's witnessed a number of global financial crises – in Mexico, Asia and Russia - that rocked the world's financial markets.

The stabilization package that was implemented in Mexico in 1995 achieved its intended results - but at a huge cost – not to the country's corrupt elites or foreign lenders, but to the country's middle class and poor. The resulting recession caused a reduction in average wages of almost 15%.

Fallout from the Asian financial crisis of 1997 had the same effect. Thailand's unemployment rate doubled. In Indonesia millions lost their jobs, and at the same time the prices of basic staples like chicken and rice rose by nearly 100%, resulting in riots in the streets.

While the financial markets are seen as the playground for the rich and

---

[29] Jeffrey D. Sachs, *The End of Poverty*, (New York: The Penguin Press, 2005).
[30] Ibid.

famous, when the markets fail, it is frequently the middle-class and poor who are most affected. The International Monetary Fund (IMF) provides economic remedies, where the cure for the disease is often worse than the illness itself. The IMF understands this and is attempting to move away from a 'one size fits all' approach. They are modifying their concept of conditionality (i.e. the terms and conditions of their financial assistance) by both reducing the number of conditions and focusing on those actions that are required for macroeconomic stability and growth. This has been accompanied recently by a greater degree of transparency in the work and activities of the IMF. Both these developments are positive.

At meetings of the Parliamentary Network of the World Bank in Athens in March 2003, Mr. Horst Köhler, who was at that time the Managing Director of the IMF, stressed that the geopolitics of the times (e.g. tension in Iraq) were bad for business investment and consumer spending. These factors lead to lackluster economic growth which results in reduced development assistance. He spoke about the need for more economic growth in Europe and for structural reforms in countries like Japan. He mentioned that trade barriers, particularly in agriculture, limit growth in developing countries, and that world leaders need to develop a more thoughtful policy framework to deal with globalization. The two downsides of globalization, in his view are that too many people will be left behind, together with the risk of financial crisis.

Mr. Köhler discussed the need for balance between human rights and human responsibilities amongst:
- the markets;
- social equity; and
- individual responsibility to society and the common good.

He indicated that the IMF is in the process of change, including:
- greater transparency;
- working on rules and standards of the game by encouraging standards and codes (e.g. money laundering);
- focused on financial sector (strengths and weaknesses);
- changed concept of conditionality by reducing the number of conditions and focusing on those key areas that are required for macroeconomic stability and growth.

He concluded by emphasizing the following priorities for the IMF:
- sustained growth;
- international stability;
- addressing poverty; and,
- the IMF becoming a learning institution (i.e. they don't have all the answers).

At these same meetings, we had a useful dialogue with Mr. James Wolfensohn, the President of the World Bank at that time. Mr. Wolfensohn indicated the two key challenges currently considered priorities by the World Bank are the following:

1. Increasing the level of Overseas Development Assistance (ODA).

The United Nations has set a target of 0.7% of GDP as the target for developed countries. To put matters into context, Mr. Wolfensohn cited the following:

- Five percent of the world's population shares in 20% of world GDP;
- Current levels of ODA total US$52 billion, which can be contrasted with US$311 in agricultural assistance worldwide, and US$90 billion in defence spending;
- Increasing the amounts that developed countries commit to international aid is more easily accomplished when the world economy is strong and stable.

2. Improving access to markets for developing countries by reducing or eliminating tariff and non-tariff barriers.

Mr. Wolfensohn also cited some continuing areas of concern/action:

- combating HIV/AIDS;
- fighting corruption by building capacity and pushing for legal and judicial reform;
- supporting education, health and infrastructure projects; and,
- promoting improved interaction with the private sector and civil

society.

The run on the Thai baht, which essentially precipitated the Asian financial crisis of 1997, is an interesting and important phenomenon to examine, especially since it was preceded by a period of unprecedented economic growth in that country. Some argue that the problem was more technical in nature. (A run on the currency by speculators, which caused a severe downward spiral, resulting in the devaluation of the baht.) Accepting this theory leads one to consider policy measures, like the Tobin tax, aimed at reducing speculative flows in currencies.

In 1972, James Tobin introduced the idea of having a small tax on international transactions. His idea stemmed from the volatile reality of financial markets, which are notorious for being characterized by a surge in buying, followed by a panic of selling which results in market crashes.[31] This has been especially harmful for people of the developing world, as seen with the Mexican peso crisis of 1994-5 and the Asian crisis of 1997-98.[32] In both these instances, the volatility of the financial market left these nations with high unemployment and stunted development.

Tobin's argument for a Currency Transaction Tax (CTT) rests on its ability to create stability, efficiency and self-determination of nations.[33] First, Tobin has proposed a CTT of 0.5 percent, which would stabilize markets by preventing speculators from buying and then quickly reselling large amounts of foreign currency. Secondly, to ensure efficiency, the proposed CTT would also be highest for short-term holdings and lowest for long-term investments, encouraging investors to make long-term commitments in these countries that are desperately needed for continued development.

Tobin also argues that the tax will prevent the IMF's 'one size fits all' way of dealing with lenders, which left countries such as Mexico, during the Peso crisis, in a depression with high unemployment and 60%

---

[31] Tobin, James, *The Tobin Tax on International Monetary Transactions.* (Ottawa: Canadian Centre for Policy Alternatives, 1995).

[32] Joy Kennedy, "Currency Transaction Tax: Curbing Speculation, Funding Social Development," *Civilizing Globalization: A Survival Guide,* ed. Richard Sandbrook. (Albany, New York: Stat University of New York Press, 2003).

[33] Patomaki, Heikki, *Democratizing Globalization: The leverage of the Tobin Tax.* (London: Zed Books, 2001).

interest rates. The CTT however, would be adaptable: if a country finds its currency threatened it could raise its CTT to a higher level to counteract the speculators, instead of raising interest rates. Such was the case in Chile who, during the 1980s, faced a current account deficit and an over-valued exchange rate. Rather than raise interest rates, the country implemented a transaction tax of 1.5% on incoming investment, resulting in an economic recovery and so averting a Mexican-like crisis.

Finally, it is argued that the Tobin Tax will help spread the ideal of democracy by giving those whose lives are most affected by the consequences of financial outcomes a greater say in financial transactions. This promotes the fundamental principle of democracy and self-determination. Unless citizens of each nation feel they have a stake in their economy, they will resist reforms necessary to develop. The revenues made from the CTT would empower nations to help themselves. Proponents of the Tobin Tax suggest that half the revenues from the CTT, (the revenues from just a 0.1 percent CCT is estimated to be over US $200 billion), would provide enough money to developing nations to aid poverty eradication and social development – with money still left over for environmental protection.

Opposition to the Tobin tax comes from nations who fear the tax will restrict their freedom. Countries that would lose from a CTT are nations such as Switzerland who have harboured offshore facilities as tax havens, and have established a reputation of 'money laundering sanctuaries' since the 1930s. More significant however is the US and UK opposition to the tax. Thatcher's implementation of the UK Banking Act removed all distinction between offshore and onshore markets, which transformed the UK into a crucial market with ex-British colonies such as Bermuda and the Cayman Islands as important offshore markets. This, coupled with the expansion of the New York market, has resulted in London and New York accounting for almost half of the world's foreign exchange since the year 2000. Unfortunately, the enormous influence of the US and the UK has meant that their opposition to the Tobin Tax is an opposition for all.

To get cooperation from nations on the tax, Tobin suggests making it a condition of membership to the IMF. In doing this, agreement among the members to levy the tax would result in the IMF acting as the administrator and establishing the rules of conduct. Tobin suggests that the wealthiest countries such as the UK the US, Germany and Japan would earmark most of what they collect in revenues for 'international purposes', such as financing the United Nations Development Program. Others argue, the IMF lacks legitimacy for governing the Tobin Tax, and the way to garner cooperation between nations is to create a new organization called the Tobin Tax Organization (TTO) which would be an independent body that collects and allocates the revenues from the tax.

In any event, co-operation among some nations has already begun. In Canada for instance, a campaign led by the Halifax Initiative (a coalition of environment, development and social justices groups) gave support to MP Lorne Nystrom's 1998 motion in the House of Commons, which encouraged the government to enact a tax on financial transactions in agreement with the international community. A signed Citizen's Declaration on the Tobin Tax was presented to Finance Minister Paul Martin, and the motion was passed in March, 1999 with a vote of 164-83 in favour of the bill. Canada became the first country in the world to announce its intention to work towards adapting the Tobin Tax. With the continued cooperation of other countries, the Tobin Tax has the ability to empower the vulnerable and lead the path towards economic and democratic changes in the developing world. The real challenge is to ensure that, if the Tobin Tax is enacted, all countries adopt it – otherwise transactions will be directed to those jurisdictions where the tax is not in place. This is the real challenge with the Tobin Tax – making it universal.

Other international taxes to fight world poverty have been discussed and proposed. More recently, France, Brazil and Chile got together with UN Secretary-General Kofi Annan to promote a global tax, levied by the airline industry, to combat world poverty. A declaration was signed in the summer of 2005 by 110 mostly developing countries supporting this tax which would augment the overseas development assistance coming from countries around the world. While this idea has some merit, the way it is proposed could hurt an already damaged airline industry which is only beginning to recover from the events of 9/11.

Coming back to Thailand, I tilt to the view that the problems in that country in 1997/98 were more fundamental in nature – especially their macroeconomic position – but more particularly the extent of cronyism in their banking system. By cronyism in this context I mean the granting of loans based on relationships, and the creation of private personal advantage, over rational lending policies. This invariably leads to bad loans (Japan is another good example of this), followed by huge write-downs and losses.

In the late 1980's I had the opportunity to stay with some Canadian friends in Thailand. These friends had lived in Thailand for some years, so they knew the area well. I had the opportunity to play golf with a retired deputy minister in the Thai government. He was a very genial fellow and we had an enjoyable round of golf. On the way to the golf course, we were pulled over for speeding – a very common occurrence in Thailand. The police constable came over to the rolled-down window of our car and showed off a very large and impressive book of speeding tickets. Our driver sorted the whole affair out in a few minutes with a bribe in lieu of the bother of writing up a ticket. I was told that tickets are rarely, if ever, issued by police officers in circumstances like this. Police officers are paid extremely low wages and are expected to make most of their income through bribes. It is the accepted practice. I wondered at the time why the government didn't pay better wages and use the ticket revenue to defray the costs – perhaps a small step towards mitigating the culture and psychology of bribery.

As I said, I had the chance when in Thailand to play a round of golf with a retired Deputy Minister – an individual who had had a very successful career in the public service of Thailand. Having spent much of my career before politics in the forest sector, I enquired about the recent ban on logging in Thailand. Earlier that year torrential rains and floods had virtually wiped out a number of villages in Thailand which precipitated the ban. Logging and over-cutting were blamed for most of these mishaps. My golfing partner told me that in northern Thailand the logging concessionaires were very accommodating with the government forestry officers. They were frequently told that their options were two-fold when presented with a logging plan for approval. They could either accept the logging plan (which was made easier with a handsome bribe) or enjoy a float down a local river as a corpse! The result, not surprisingly, are massive areas denuded by clear cuts with little or no consideration of land erosion or soil impacts. I was told that the Thailand Forest Service offices in Bangkok were the most opulent of all government departments. I presumed that some of the forest industry largesse found its way through these channels as well.

Years later, while employed by a major forest industry company in Canada, I was invited by the Chairman to a meeting with a visiting delegation from Thailand. The individual leading the delegation was Secretary to the Queen Mother in Thailand. It is important to note that the royal family in Thailand is very much respected and revered by the citizens of that country. They are akin to our government ombudsman, and are expected to look after the interests of the 'little guy'. Other senior government officials accompanied the Secretary. In Thailand's continuing quest to replace drug crops, the royal family had converted former drug crop sites to tree plantations with groundnuts as the short-term cash crop. Similar experiments had been attempted in the past, but the sites had converted back to drug crops within a year. The temptation of the high paying, cash yielding drug crops had been too hard to resist. Given the short growing cycle for trees in Thailand (especially when compared with countries like Canada), and the fact that the local population had left the trees intact – a testimony to the respect expressed for royal projects – the trees were ready for harvesting. The Thai Royal Family were looking to major forest products companies in North America to build a pulp mill or panel board mill to process the harvested logs. As a company we were interested, but never had the opportunity to consummate the deal as a result of a coup which followed their visit to Canada – one of many coups in that country!

Considering all these examples and arguments, is it possible to avoid this type of major financial and economic collapse? This is a tall order perhaps, given the complexity and size of the challenge. Initiatives have been launched by the international community (e.g. the G-20 Finance Ministers), and others are being debated.

With the encouragement and support of Rt. Hon. Paul Martin, P.C., M.P., then Canada's Minister of Finance, the Group of Twenty (G-20) Finance Ministers and Central Bank Governors was established in 1999 to bring together systemically important industrialized and developing economies. The G-20 was created as a response both to the financial crises of the late 1990s and a growing recognition that key emerging-market countries were not adequately included in the core of global economic discussion and governance. The inaugural meeting of the G-20 took place in Berlin on 15-16 December 1999, hosted by the German and Canadian finance ministers.

The members of the G-20 are the finance ministers and central bank governors of 19 countries: Argentina, Australia, Brazil, Canada, China, France, Germany, India, Indonesia, Italy, Japan, Mexico, Russia, Saudi Arabia, South Africa, South Korea, Turkey, the United Kingdom and the United States of America. The European Union is also a member, represented by the rotating Council presidency and the European Central Bank. Together, member countries represent around 90 per cent of the global gross national product, 80 per cent of world trade (including EU intra-trade) as well as two-thirds of the world's population. The G-20's economic weight and broad membership gives it a high degree of legitimacy and influence over the management of the global economy and financial system.

While the G-20 started out as a forum for Finance Ministers, Paul Martin promoted the idea of expanding the concept to the level of first Ministers (i.e. Prime Ministers, Heads of State). The G-20 will assist in anticipating, and preparing for, international financial crises. As well, it is engaged in preventative work by proactively putting in place the policies and institutions necessary for good governance and sound fiscal and monetary policy in countries around the world.

CHAPTER 2

MONEY LAUNDERING AND THE FINANCING OF TERRORISM

Parliamentarians who I have met from around the world who are concerned about corruption, and fighting to do something about it, view money laundering as inextricably linked to the challenge of reducing or eliminating corruption. Those in corrupt countries become very discouraged in their fight against corruption when corrupt funds are easily and readily transferred offshore to numbered bank accounts. So, we need to deal with both issues simultaneously if we are to have a real impact.

The linkage amongst money laundering, international development assistance, and terrorism is more complicated. US Congressman Barney Frank told a May 10/11, 2003 Parliamentary Network of the World Bank conference that it is a mistake to justify more foreign aid using the security argument that more aid will make for a safer world. He suggested that this rationalization could attract a 'belligerent rather than a benevolent response' from donor countries like the United States.

What the linkage is between poverty and terrorism is unclear. However, the terrorist attacks targeted at innocent Americans by Muslim extremists on September 11th 2001 cannot be justified using any reasonable criteria. While the immediate and medium-term response must be, and has been, an outright attack on terrorism, we should also be asking ourselves – why? What motivated the perpetrators to commit themselves to certain death? What cause or purpose motivated them to make the ultimate sacrifice? Commentators and experts have advanced various hypotheses. These people are Islamic fundamentalists who are determined to destabilize the

United States for political reasons, say some. The individuals, say others, are responding to the call for a Jihad against the impure and against the excesses of western society. Islamists have attacked the American way of life. Yossef Bodansky suggests that: "Followers of the Ayatollah Khomeini in Iran view the United States as a land preoccupied with the adulation and worship of money, and Majid Anaraki, an Iranian who lived for several years in southern California, described the United States as a 'collection of casinos, supermarkets, and whore-houses linked together by endless highways passing through nowhere', all dominated and motivated by the lust for money."[34] Still others speculate that the motivation is to draw attention to the plight of the Palestinians. Many theories abound.

In his book, *Cold Terror*, Stewart Bell argues that "The root cause of Islamic terrorism is not poverty, nor is it, as Chrétien has also suggested, Western arrogance and greed – it is that a group of fanatics wants to convince Muslims that theirs is the one true faith and that it is their duty and right to take over the world by force."[35]

"…Europeans prefer to say that the root cause of terrorism is poverty – or the unresolved conflict in Palestine, which they accuse Mr. Bush of having dangerously neglected during his first term."[36] President George Bush argues that the primary cause of terrorism is the failure of democracy to take root in the Middle East.

While we may never know the real motivation for such terrorist actions (indeed the individuals involved may not know clearly why they did what they did!) in my view, the reasons for this type of behaviour are more profound and more fundamental. It has to do with the growing impatience and frustration by those who 'don't have', in contrast with those who 'have'. I believe it is derived from the classical 'have/have-not' tension.

Former U.S. President Bill Clinton, in his autobiographical book, *My Life,* asserts that one of the five priorities that the United States should be pursuing is to "…make more friends and fewer terrorists by helping the 50 per cent of the world not reaping the benefits of globalization to overcome

---

[34] Yossesf Bodansky, *Bin Laden – The Man Who Declared War on America*, Prima Publishing, 1999; page XIII-XIV

[35] Stewart Bell, *Cold Terror*, Stewart Bell. (John Wiley & Sons Canada Ltd. 2004).

[36] *The Economist*, February 19 2005, p. 11.

poverty, ignorance, disease and bad government..."[37]

Economic crimes, such as money laundering and corruption, are a threat to the development of new market economies and democratic principles and, because they are trans-national in nature, they are rightly dealt with by multilateral organizations.

The financing of terrorist activities, and related money laundering activities, threatens the peaceful co-existence of countries and people around the world. The events of September 11 2001 clearly demonstrated this.

In 1998 I was pleased to address the Parliamentary Assembly of the Council of Europe in Strasbourg on the topic of economic crimes. I was told at that time by my Liberal colleague and long-standing President of the Canada-Europe Parliamentary Association, Charles Caccia, that I was the first Canadian Parliamentarian to address the Parliamentary Assembly of the Council of Europe. I was very honoured to do this, but also quite intimidated, especially because two speakers ahead of me was Vladimir Zhirinovsky, the ultra-nationalist Leader of the Liberal Democrats in Russia at that time, and one-time Russian Presidential candidate. During his speech he lashed out at a pregnant delegate in the Chamber of the Parliamentary Assembly, and told those assembled that the delegate's child would be born in the form of a devil because of the mother's views on a certain topic!

In my closing remarks, I said the following:

"In Canada, more can and will be done, but we are moving in the right direction. Unfortunately, many eastern Europeans are witnessing the very worst side of a market-based economy. Wealth oligarchies have been created very fast and in many cases have been coupled with coercive elements. The results have often been disastrous. Average citizens feel victimized and unable to participate in the emerging market economy – they feel left out. For the original skeptics, that provides support for their argument that the old ways are better."

"The real issue is how long those who feel victimized and excluded will wait before their patience runs out. The goal of a market economy coupled with democratic principles is to create a more inclusive society,

---

[37] Bill Clinton. *My Life (The Presidential Years),* (Vintage Books, 2005).

not the other way around. To be sure, a perfect world is not possible under any system, but we must develop and put in place the governance models that will achieve the needed results."

"In my view, the challenge in Eastern Europe is to limit as quickly as possible the growth of mafia-like activities so as to allow all citizens the opportunity to improve their economic prospects. In our role as parliamentarians, I am confident that we can work together constructively and effectively to make that change."

Since I made those remarks much has changed, but much, regrettably, has remained the same. I believe the challenges I described in Strasbourg still exist.

Money laundering and corruption are unfortunate 'bed-partners'. It is estimated that worldwide money laundering approaches $1 trillion per year (about the same size as Canada's entire GDP!). The proceeds from corruption and other crimes are often laundered to make the funds more accessible to the perpetrators. Corruption is often associated with organized crime. Effective anti-money laundering regimes have the effect of constraining corrupt activities as there are fewer outlets and means to benefit from these crimes. The chain, however, is only as strong as its weakest link, and this is why it is important for all countries to implement effective anti-money laundering regimes.

The downing of passenger airlines in Russia in August 2004 by terrorists also highlights how corruption and terrorism can be linked. It is alleged that the terrorist who blew up one of the planes was initially denied boarding the aircraft because of some irregularities with her documentation. A bribe approximating US$50 was paid – allowing her to board the aircraft and eventually blow up the aircraft, causing the death of 46 people.

In my work on the fight against corruption and money laundering, it has been pointed on a number of occasions by parliamentarians in corrupt countries that they understand the need for, and they are committed to the fight against corruption, but they cannot help but become dismayed and discouraged when they witness the unimpeded flight of corrupt funds from their country to 'safe havens'. They are right to be concerned because it is only by fighting both corruption and money laundering activities that any success can be achieved. Slowing down or eliminating the laundering of corrupt money will seriously serve as a disincentive to corrupt activities.

In the fight against the laundering of corrupt funds, something else is very clear. The world must act together to stamp out money laundering everywhere. The old adage 'the chain is as good as its weakest link' very much applies here. As the Minister of Finance for Swaziland, the Honourable Majozi Sithole, pointed out at a 2003 conference: "Money laundering can only be fully addressed by countries collectively, as criminals operate without regard to national boundaries. Any weak links in the anti-money laundering chain will be exploited."[38]

In the late 1990's the OECD launched an initiative labelled the fight against harmful tax competition. It originally began as an attack on offshore banking centers like those found in the Bahamas, Switzerland, Luxembourg and other locations. The primary concern initially was focused on the growing trend for funds in the industrialized economies of member countries of the OECD to find their way to offshore banking centers as a means of evading taxes. Once it became clear that it was difficult, if not impossible, to determine what level of taxation, per se, was competitively harmful, the focus of this exercise shifted to a demand for greater transparency from the offshore banking centers, or tax havens. It became highly judgmental for example, to make a reasonable assessment whether or not the rates of taxation in a country like Ireland, where corporate and individual income tax rates are low, are harmful and non-competitive. It may well be that the rates in Ireland are set at a very appropriate level, and those in other countries in the industrialized world set at levels that are too high. It is fair, however, to insist on greater transparency and better disclosure so that those taxpayers that are suspected of evading taxes in their home country can be examined and their financial structure and transactions subjected to greater scrutiny.

Achieving this greater transparency in tax havens is a daunting task. Countries like Switzerland have built their reputations on the confidentiality of client information. Recent interest in terrorist financing activities has had the result of improving tax haven transparency. Proceeds from crime

---

[38] Monograph: *Profiling Money Laundering in Eastern and Southern Africa*, Edited by Charles Goredema, Executive Summary.

– especially drug trafficking funds – elicit greater cooperation from tax haven authorities. It is still more difficult, however, for tax havens to be more forthcoming with information when tax evasion and corrupt activities are the primary concern – but progress is being made.

Over the years I have found it somewhat curious that whenever I have spoken to groups of parliamentarians about the need to fight corruption and money laundering it has generated much interest and subsequent follow-up. The most vociferous are those elected individuals from jurisdictions like Luxembourg and Switzerland. Needless to say, they are at the opposite end of the debate and they make great attempts to describe the measures their countries have implemented to combat money laundering. In one sense, they are correct in that post 9/11 offshore banking centers and tax havens are co-operating more fully with law enforcement agencies and intelligence operations. The level of co-operation, however, as it relates to the laundering of corrupt money still leaves much to be desired.

Tracing corrupt funds can be a daunting task since the audit trail in most cases is highly complex and convoluted. What is a corrupt activity in one country may not be considered such in another country. After the break-up of the former Soviet Union in the early 1990's, Russia embarked on an aggressive program of privatization. Many of these privatizations, however, were corrupt by western standards. Certain individuals and groups, or so-called political elites, were provided with advantages in the privatization processes. The Executive Branch of the Russian government sanctioned these processes. Were the funds that eventually flowed offshore (some to Canada) from the profits of these 'bent' privatizations considered corrupt funds? This is a moot point. The criterion used in Canada's anti-money laundering regime is that, to be considered proceeds from crime, the offence would have to be a criminal offence under the laws of Canada. So would the proceeds from a 'bent' privatization in Russia qualify? There is no easy answer. The examples flow in many other countries. What is legal in Brazil may be illegal in Canada, and perhaps vice versa. How does one prove the source of the funds given the typical cover-up of the trail?

Canada's federal government has a very active program (through the Canadian International Development Agency and the Parliamentary

Centre) working with Russia to assist them in the development of their democratic institutions and improving their governance. I had the opportunity to meet with members of the State Duma (the lower chamber), the Federation Council (the upper chamber), and the Accounts Chamber of the Russian Federation (equivalent of Canada's Auditor General), for the exchange of information on the role of the Budget Committee, the Public Accounts Committee and the Auditor General. Russia is trying to develop its democratic institutions and a market economy in a country that has no such history or experience. Before the collapse of communism in the late 1980's, Russia had experienced an almost unique history of totalitarian rule – from the Tsars, to dictators like Lenin and Stalin.

The Soviet Union and Eastern Europe chose the 'big bang' approach to reform following the demise of communism. I happened to be in Moscow in 1991 when Boris Yeltsin bolted from the Communist Party, challenging Gorbachev. The politics in the country at that time were very fluid – and that continues to this day.

The 'big bang' theory emphasized the need for simultaneous changes to the economy, political institutions and the system of law and contracts. This contrasts with China's strategy of piece-meal and carefully sequenced reforms. In terms of industrial strategy, "Mikhail Gorbachev's early programs emphasized massive equipment imports, building more machines, intensified use of machine tools, organization of industry under super ministries, improvement of the of the petroleum industry, and reorganization of the automobile and high-technology sectors. All of these are capital-intensive industries........but these failed policies also owe much to a premature emphasis on privatizing giant state enterprises which was encouraged by West European and (especially) American professors."[39]

China's amazing economic growth in recent years has caused the leadership in China to implement strategies that will give them more control over raw materials, especially commodities that are needed to fuel this growth. For Canada this has meant interest by the People's Republic of China in some strategic assets in this country. I have raised some concerns about the use of Chinese state-owned enterprises in such transactions.

---

[39] Overholt, William H., *The Rise of China*. (W.W. Norton & Company Inc., 1995).

The following letter which I wrote to the editor of the National Post was published on October 14 2004.

> **Re: Noranda Inc. takeover by the People's Republic of China**
>
> Dear Editor:
>
> The proposed takeover of Noranda Inc. by China Minmetals Corp., a Chinese state-owned enterprise, is, I submit, not about human rights practices and labour codes in the Peoples' Republic of China. While I respect the concerns of others on this theme, the reality is that if the developed countries of the world applied this benchmark to all of our trade and investment relationships, I am afraid we would fall short in many other instances. By way of contrast, I am a supporter of engagement - because I believe that a strong economy in countries like the Peoples' Republic of China will be the fertile ground for the development of more progressive social policies in those countries.
>
> So why shouldn't our government approve this takeover?
>
> The somewhat unique characteristic of this takeover is that China Minmetals Corp. is a state-owned enterprise. For me that raises a whole new set of questions.
>
> Is it appropriate for a government to take control of any operating company - in particular outside their own jurisdiction? Is this one of their core businesses? What do they know about mining? What do they bring to the table? How can any synergies be realized?

This acquisition is designed to meet a policy objective of the national government in the Peoples' Republic of China. One can only presume that, given the current high cost of commodities like minerals and metals, their desire is to 'backward integrate' and acquire control and ownership of this element of their raw material supply chain. To their credit, the economy in the Peoples' Republic of China is growing at an incredible rate. A consequence of this is the current upward price pressures on oil and other commodities (good news for Canada!).

If Noranda is acquired by China Minmetals Corp. will the company be managed in an environmentally sustainable way and in interest of all Noranda stakeholders (e.g. Noranda workers, communities where Noranda operates, the citizens of Canada, other Noranda shareholders, etc.)? I believe it is naïve to think that the government in China and China Minmetals Corp. will be 'hands-off' in the management of Noranda. It is not their style.

If they own and control Noranda, won't they be tempted, within the bounds of international trade laws and Canada's own transfer pricing tax policies, to have differential pricing for the sale of metals and minerals to strategically important operations in China? Who knows what their game plan is? Count on it, though, to be very well thought out and very shrewd.

My concern is that while this acquisition might be in the public interest in China, it is less clear to me what the benefit is for Canada.

Interestingly, in the 1980's, the Japanese government orchestrated an over-supply of metallurgical coal to feed their struggling steel mills, by partnering and investing in the northeast coal project in British Columbia. Guess what - an oversupply puts downward pressure on prices! Is that the goal of the Peoples' Republic of China for metals and minerals? If so, how does that align with Canada's interests?

> Industry Canada's Investment Review Division will allow a takeover to proceed if it provides a significant benefit to Canada. They have yet to veto a major takeover of a Canadian company. Perhaps that is because every takeover has been in Canada's best interest. I am not so sure, and even less sure about this one. Industry Canada should have a very close look at this proposed acquisition.
>
> Like most Canadians, I am a strong nationalist in that I take great pride in our national culture and heritage and in our national institutions. I understand the need, however, to be pragmatic in recognizing that we live in a global economy and, in general terms, we need to encourage the flow of international trade and investment. It is also clear to me that Canada's relationship with the Peoples' Republic of China is a very important one.
>
> These facts, however, shouldn't blur our pursuit of Canada's overarching public policy interests. Unless other facts come to light, this takeover should be rejected on that basis.

I raised the topic of Russia's move to a market economy once with Russia's Ambassador to Canada at a dinner in Ottawa a few years ago, and he strenuously disagreed with me that westerners had influenced their country's choice of the 'big bang' approach. I suppose national pride was getting in the way; however, the alternative might be less attractive, i.e. that the Russians made the wrong choices on their own.

Despite some of the recent retrograde centralizing actions of President Putin, the Russians have been working very hard to learn how to build their democratic institutions. Their Accounts Chamber is gaining rapidly in its ability to hold the Executive Branch of the government to account. When I asked them, however, on one of their visits to Canada, if they would ever conduct an audit of a privatization transaction to assess whether or not the process had been fair, transparent and whether or not the government received fair value in the circumstances, I could never get a straight answer from the Accounts Chamber auditors. I was curious about privatizations, because in the 1990's many of these transactions in Russia were renowned for the way in which privatizations were steered towards friends of the government at very low prices. I had to conclude that the auditors weren't quite ready for such an adventure yet. Keep in mind though that it wasn't that many years ago when the Accounts Chamber reported to the Russian Tsar. They were probably not in the habit of submitting damning audit reports to the Tsar – if they valued their lives. Better governance is developing slowly but surely, but it will take time to evolve.

There is an anomaly in the way the State Duma representation is structured. Someone with a shady past and with the possibility of criminal or civil charges being brought against them, can, upon their election to the State Duma, receive the protection of this institution and escape prosecution – at least while they are elected. This type of circumstance does not bode well for attracting people of integrity – those committed to good governance and fighting corruption.

Corrupt money can be laundered in a variety of ingenious ways. In the April 10, 2004 edition of the National Post, it was reported that Zimbabwe's Finance Minister, Christopher Kuruneri, was building a 10,000 square foot home in an exclusive area just outside of Cape Town, South Africa. The cost of the house is estimated at $6 million once completed. "Among the many interesting aspects of this tale is that Mr. Kuruneri is responsible for Zimbabwe's foreign currency laws, which place strict limits on the export of the country's limited supply."[40] Of course, the Finance Minister argues that he is building this home using funds that he accumulated in the private sector before his election – funds that stayed outside of Zimbabwe and therefore not subject to the foreign currency rules. Not a totally implausible story, but in sharp contrast to other theories that the house is actually being built for his boss, Robert Mugabe!

As Parliamentary Secretary to Canada's Minister of Finance from 1999 to 2001, I had the responsibility and honour to shepherd our government's anti-money laundering legislation through our parliament. This legislation, the *Proceeds of Crime (Money Laundering) and Terrorist Financing Act*, which was initially enacted in 2000, led to the creation of Canada's anti-money laundering agency, the Financial Transactions & Reports Analysis Centre (FINTRAC), which started up in November, 2001. FINTRAC is

---

[40] Kelly McParland. April 10 2004. *National Post*.

currently monitoring any suspicious financial transactions, as defined by regulation and guidelines. In October 2001 FINTRAC was given added responsibilities and resources to combat the financing of terrorist activities in Canada. Canada is now largely compliant with the anti-terrorism financing standards announced by the Financial Action Task Force, the G-7 institution that combats money laundering..

Canada's Auditor General has been somewhat critical of FINTRAC in three principal areas:

- the exclusion of lawyers from the reporting requirements of 'suspicious' transactions;
- the provision of 'tombstone data' only in the first instance to law enforcement agencies;
- the lack of measurable results.

I will deal with each criticism in turn. First, the government, in passing the *Proceeds of Crime* legislation and establishing FINTRAC included all financial intermediaries, including lawyers. The view then and now is that the net should be as broad as can be on the theory that 'a chain is as good as its weakest link'. If lawyers had been excluded initially, money launderers would have been attracted to this avenue as a vehicle for their laundering activities. Unfortunately, the Canadian Bar Association successfully challenged the legislation on the basis of solicitor-client privilege. Finance (Canada) is currently negotiating with Canada's lawyers to determine if some negotiated solution is possible.

The second critique of the Auditor General stems from the requirements of Canada's *Privacy Act*. Transactions that are considered suspicious are summarized in a high-level (or tombstone) form so that the confidentiality of Canadians is respected. If law enforcement agencies, based on their information and analysis, concur with FINTRAC that the transactions warrant further investigation, they must present their case to a Federal Court Judge who will then decide if more detailed information can be released to the police. Without these protections, the law would likely have been struck down as being offside to Canada's *Privacy Act*.

Measuring results and evaluating the effectiveness of FINTRAC is a daunting task, but one that must be pursued. Can one realistically link data supplied from FINTRAC to law enforcement agencies in Canada to ultimate arrests and convictions? With the passage of time, more of this will be able to be done; however, the connections are in some cases tenuous.

FINTRAC is reviewed by Parliament every five years, which is a requirement of the Act, at which time parliamentarians can examine questions posed by the Auditor General carefully. Perhaps a better balance of privacy interests and the enforcement of money laundering offences can be struck.

The Financial Action Task Force on Money Laundering (FATF) is an inter-governmental body whose purpose is the development and promotion of policies to combat money laundering; the processing of criminal proceeds in order to disguise their illegal origin. These policies aim to prevent such proceeds from being utilized in future criminal activities and from affecting legitimate economic activities. Interestingly, Canada took on the Presidency of the FATF in the summer of 2006. Frank Swetlove, a former senior Finance Canada official, performed a great job in that role.

The FATF currently consists of 29 countries and two international organizations. Its membership includes the major financial center countries of Europe, North and South America, and Asia. The Global Organization of Parliamentarians Against Corruption (GOPAC) has identified the fight against money laundering as a priority of the organization. I have been asked to lead this initiative by bringing together a team of twelve or so parliamentarians from around the world – those interested in fighting money laundering.

The objectives of this initiative are:
a) to engage parliamentarians from around the world in the anti-money laundering (AML) agenda by developing a better understanding of how money laundering occurs and launching an international initiative to combat it; and
b) to build political support to effectively implement practical mechanisms to combat money laundering.

The ultimate result that GOPAC is seeking to extend the anti-money laundering regime beyond its current focus – principally in Europe and North America, and to develop effective strategies that parliamentarians can execute (e.g. promotion of international treaties) to combat money laundering.

The GOPAC Team will work with AML experts and organizations (such as the Financial Action Task Force (FATF) associated with the OECD, and the International Monetary Fund) to develop an approach to combating money laundering and promote its practical implementation.

GOPAC's approach to building integrity in governance is to bring together political will and expertise to empower parliamentarians in all countries. Such an approach, especially on a matter where there are regional differences and sensitivities, takes time to develop the necessary understanding, build consensus and guide implementation.

GOPAC proposes, therefore, to begin by ensuring that the Team fully understands the current international approach and its implications before beginning to assess the impediments and special features of their regions that could hinder or require adjustments prior to implementation. These will be documented for discussion and resolution. After such background work, the Team will shift its focus to developing a coherent global strategy that is sensitive to these differences and develop an approach to implementing a global AML regime. This includes developing tools and supporting materials for parliamentarians. The final step is communicating the approach internationally, including through GOPAC. We anticipate that GOPAC would formally adopt the approach and lead its implementation.

The work will proceed through four distinct stages:

1) Orientation and Training: Building a knowledgeable team of parliamentarians to work with the international organizations that are developing Anti-Money Laundering Initiatives (AMLI); to provide political support and motivation; to increase public awareness of the need for AMLI; and to bring AMLI to a successful conclusion in many parts of the world.

2) Development of Position and Discussion Papers: In association with the organizations participating in AMLI: to publish position and discussion papers; to engage GOPAC members and parliamentarians in general around the world; to raise awareness of AMLI; and to coalesce parliamentary opinion on the issue.

Team members will work within their regions to provide a broad-based understanding of current practices and issues.

3) Prepare and Publish a Report: In association with the organizations participating in AMLI, to publish a substantive document, within the next two to three years, outlining objectives desired. These could include an international treaty or convention, making acceptance of laundered money by a financial institution a crime in their own country – and the repatriation of the money should it occur. The document will include significant detail and set out the way ahead.

4) Conference: To host a conference of parliamentarians (GOPAC members) to sell the substantive document and the way ahead with follow-up by GOPAC and its chapters to motivate and monitor progress.

Money laundering is a device for making illegally obtained funds accessible for the personal use of perpetrators without being traceable back to their illicit source – typically by transferring the funds across international borders to legitimate financial institutions. The central concept of Anti-money Laundering Initiatives (AMLI) is to reduce the motivation for economic crimes by making more difficult access to their proceeds.

AMLI initiatives are important to discourage the supply of funds to international terrorists and their organizations. Impeding the international flow of such funds reduces the means available to terrorists and identifying their sources discourages their funders.

The negative effects of corruption are obvious. Some of the poorest countries in the world are the most corrupt, as measured by Transparency International's Global Corruption Report. According to Transparency International a one unit decline on a 10-point corruption index lowers real GDP by 0.3 to 1.8 percentage points. Looked at from the perspective of an individual firm, bribery adds to the cost of doing business (in Uganda, an estimated 8%).

The principal global initiative to reduce money laundering to date has been the formation of the Financial Action Task Force (FATF) in 1991 by the G-7 (Group of Seven Countries). FATF is closely associated with the OECD and its members, and its secretariat is located in the OECD offices in Paris. It recommends 40 actions – recently updated – for governments. Most OECD countries have accepted these.

The recommendations include:
- making money laundering a crime;
- requiring financial institutions to: know their clients; maintain records; and exercise due diligence regarding suspicious transactions; and
- requiring governments to: monitor cross-border transport of cash and report aggregate flows to the IMF and BIS (Bank for International Settlement); ensure financial institutions have appropriate capacity; and cooperate internationally on information, investigation and prosecution.

FATF has a peer review process to assess the degree and quality of member's compliance with its recommendations.

FATF is the recognized source of expertise on money laundering. Our GOPAC project, accordingly, will establish arrangements with FATF in order to benefit from its expertise and advice. Where individual governments are willing to provide access to their experts, the project will use such services as needed. In addition, individual experts will be retained on contract to undertake needed tasks and draft the planned reports.

Parliamentarians can play a vital role through their influence on legislation, by vigorous oversight of government activity and support of parliamentary auditors, and perhaps most effectively through personal leadership. They can engage the public and help build the political will to act. However, to do so, they must understand how money laundering occurs and the mechanisms for its mitigation. They also need the support of recognized experts and a global voice. GOPAC provides the global voice and the proposed Anti-money Laundering Initiative can help provide the understanding and expertise.

The selection of parliamentarians to participate on the Team will be particularly important. The key requirements are parliamentarians with experience and a track record in the field, as well as regional balance.

Energy, political skill and gender balance also will be important for credibility and effectiveness.

Canada's parliament has also ratified the United Nations International Convention for the Suppression of the Financing of Terrorism with the enactment in December, 2001 of an Anti-terrorism bill.

These initiatives in Canada have not been without controversy. The anti-money laundering legislation raised a number of concerns with respect to privacy issues, which had to be dealt with very sensitively. Our anti-terrorism legislation raised the ire of many who believed, and still believe, that their human rights were infringed upon. This is the careful work that legislators must perform in order to achieve a balance between these sometimes competing objectives.

When enacting Canada's anti-money laundering regime, our attitude was that the reporting of transactions should extend to all financial intermediaries and all possible parties to money laundering transactions. This includes banks, foreign exchange dealers, accountants and lawyers and many other categories. The view was, and is, that any groups that were exempted would become a natural target for money launderers. Lawyers in Canada made their case to be excluded from the reporting provisions of the anti-money laundering legislation on the grounds of solicitor-client privilege. The government elected in the Act not to exclude them and they have successfully challenged this decision in the courts. It is my hope that a negotiated solution can be achieved which respects the rights of lawyers to protect their clients, but which also does not provide money launderers with a convenient route to launder the proceeds from their crimes.

I should add that Canada is a signatory to the OECD Convention on Bribery, and in 1998 passed into law the legislation necessary to implement this convention. This law is entitled *The Corruption of Foreign Public Officials Act*. Also, in 1991 Canada ended the tax deductibility of bribes in international business transactions. Surprisingly, this practice has not been eliminated in many other countries.

Led by Canada, the G-20 finance ministers and central bank governors agreed to an Action Plan on Terrorist Financing at their meeting in Ottawa on November 17 2001. This Plan commits member nations to:

- Implement the relevant United Nations Security Council

Resolutions and Conventions to freeze terrorist assets and stop the financing of terrorism;
- Work with international bodies to promote the adoption, implementation and assessment of standards to combat abuses of the financial system, including terrorist financing and money laundering;
- Provide technical assistance to countries that need help in developing and implementing necessary laws, regulations and policies to combat terrorist financing and money laundering; and
- Establish Financial Intelligence Units and facilitate the exchange of information on terrorist financing and money laundering.

Because bribery and corruption have both a demand and a supply side, it is very important for businesses to refuse to offer bribes. In this regard, the Canadian business community adopted an International Code of Ethics for Canadian business, which contains, amongst other things, a commitment to the following values: to human rights and social justice; to wealth maximization for all stakeholders; to the operation of a free market economy; and, to a business environment that mitigates against bribery and corruption.

At the 2005 session of the World Economic Forum in Davos, Switzerland, some 47 large multi-national corporations agreed to a 'zero-tolerance' pact against paying bribes. More companies are needed to sign on to this initiative, including mining and oil and gas companies who are noticeably absent. This is an important development which will grow over time. Companies will need to become accountable to their zero-tolerance commitments. With concerted action and coordinated efforts, progress can be made in limiting or eliminating the 'supply-side' of bribery and corruption.

The 1997 OECD Convention on Bribery, now signed by 35 countries states that "enterprises should not, directly or indirectly, offer, promise, give or demand a bribe or other undue advantage to obtain or retain business." Regrettably, about a third of the signatories to this OECD convention are performing below standard (including Luxembourg, Britain, Italy and Japan), a third are 'middle of the road', and a third are performing well, according to a recent assessment by the OECD. Clearly, more needs to be done to implement this Convention.

The Parliament of Canada implemented its commitment to this OECD Convention in 1999. Additional information can be located in the OECD's Report of the Implementation of the Convention in Canada: http://www.oecd.org/dataoecd/13/35/2385703.pdf

The United Nations has an important role to play in the fight against corruption and in improving the investment climate in developing countries, as I pointed out in my April 28th 2004 remarks in the 2004 Ordinary Session of the Parliamentary Assembly of the Council of Europe during the debate on Strengthening the United Nations.

"Mr. President...Canada is committed to a multilateral approach to international security and the prevention of armed conflict. This is why we decided not to participate in the war against Iraq – because there was no international consensus to act militarily at that time. The Canadian public generally was very supportive of this position – and continue to be.

The United Nations is in need of reform, however. There are times when the United Nations seemed to be paralysed into inaction. Ten years ago, hundreds of thousands of Rwandans lost their lives in genocide, while the international community failed to act. Our own Lieutenant General Romeo D'Allaire was very much at the epicentre of this tragedy. Secretary General Kofi Annan is aware of these structural and decision-making problems at the UN, and I applaud him for addressing this – especially with the High Level Panel on Threats, Challenges and Change.

Canada has promoted the human security agenda which emphasizes that the security of individuals transcends national borders and requires the international community to act if it is at risk. There is a balance here, however, that needs to be carefully maintained to ensure that the sovereignty of nations is respected.

When is it appropriate for a country, or the international community, to attempt to overthrow a despotic ruler in a failed or failing state when the personal security of citizens is threatened?

What criteria should apply?

In its reform agenda, the United Nations needs to address these vexing

questions, and design a governance model that will facilitate timely and appropriate responses when the safety and security of our fellow citizens of the world are at risk.

Reform of the UN Security Council must protect the role of middle powers – like many of the member states of the Council of Europe and Canada, while acknowledging the need for new permanent members.

The rapporteur has appropriately categorized international security issues as 'hard' threats. Equally problematic are the 'soft' threats, because as Mrs. Zulueta rightly points out these 'soft' threats are often at the origin of 'hard' threats.

While we shouldn't be naïve about ideological differences that are often at the centre of international disputes, the growing gap between the 'have' and 'have-not' nations is also at the root of the problem. Corruption however, is impeding the investment of public and private funds in developing countries – at the very moment when help is most needed. I should note the good work in the fight against corruption and money laundering being performed by the Global Organization of Parliamentarians Against Corruption, or GOPAC – an international network of over 250 Parliamentarians from 72 countries of the world, organized by region, to build integrity and promote effective governance. Canada hosted the first meeting of this group in Ottawa in October, 2002.

The area of so-called 'soft' threats is one where the United Nations can play a larger role as well – principally through the Economic and Social Council or ECOSOC. The rapporteur's suggestion to form an Economic and Social Security Council at the UN is an interesting proposition and worthy of examination.

The United Nations Convention Against Corruption and the UN Commission on the Private Sector and Development are two very important recent initiatives focused in this area – but more needs to be done.

I look forward to the reform of the United Nations and to the contribution that the Parliamentary Assembly of the Council of Europe can make to this transformation. The UN is a very important institution that deserves our full attention."

In early December 2003, the Government of Mexico hosted an international signing ceremony for the UN Convention Against Corruption (UNCAC). Over 95 countries signed on to the convention with Kenya already having ratified the UNCAC. This new convention deals with prevention and punishment of corruption in both the private and public sectors. The highlights of this Convention are as follows:

Prevention: Measures such as the establishment of anti-corruption bodies and enhanced transparency in the financing of election campaigns and political parties address both the public and private sectors. Requirements are also established for the prevention of corruption in the judiciary and in public procurement. The Convention calls on countries to actively promote the involvement of non-governmental and community-based organizations as well as other elements of civil society, to raise public awareness of corruption.

Criminalization: Countries are required to establish criminal and other offences to cover a wide range of acts of corruption. This includes not only basic forms of corruption, such as bribery and the embezzlement of public funds, but also trading in influence and the concealment and 'laundering' of the proceeds of corruption.

International Co-operation: Countries agree to co-operate in the fight against corruption, including prevention and investigation activities, and the prosecution of offenders. The Convention also binds countries to render specific forms of mutual legal assistance in gathering and transferring evidence for use in court and to extradite offenders. Countries must also undertake measures to support the tracing, freezing, seizure and confiscation of the proceeds of corruption.

Asset Recovery: This is an important issue for many developing countries where high level corruption has plundered the national wealth, and where resources are badly needed for reconstruction and the rehabilitation of societies under new governments. Measures include the prevention and detection of transfers of illicitly acquired assets, the recovery of property, and the return and disposition of assets.

CHAPTER 3

WHY CORRUPTION IS STIFLING THE FLOW OF INVESTMENT CAPITAL

The Problem of Investment

Investment capital, especially in today's global economy, is highly mobile and it will move to the projects with the best risk/return ratio, i.e. where the rate of return and the risk level are optimized. This is especially true for private capital. The public sector comes into play when the market is not responding, or not responding appropriately or adequately. The reasons for the private sector not responding could be numerous, but one obvious reason would be that the perceived risk is too high in relation to the benefit or potential return on investment. Another would be where the development project creates 'public goods' (e.g. hospitals, roads, education) where there is no discernable rent to be captured by the private sector (i.e. no private profit). This is where overseas development assistance from governments, and grants and loans from NGO's and institutions like the World Bank and the European Bank for Reconstruction and Development (EBRD) come into play to provide subsidies or bridge financing for 'public good' projects or initiatives. But the tolerance for risk for governments, public institutions and NGO's is not open ended. Risk levels must be manageable – and good governance in the jurisdiction in question plays heavily into this assessment.

James D. Wolfensohn, former President of the World Bank, has indicated that corruption is the "single largest deterrent to private sector investing."[41] Private and public investments flowing to the developing world is one way of increasing economic output, improving productivity and assisting developing countries in wealth creation. Foreign direct investment, however, will occur when perceived benefits exceed costs and where the risks are acceptable.

Professor Shang-Jin Wei of the Kennedy School of Government, Harvard University, stated that a one-grade increase in the level of corruption (as measured in this case by the International Risk Guide of the Business International Corporation – a subsidiary of the Economist Intelligence Unit) is associated with a 16% reduction in the flow of foreign direct investment – roughly equivalent to the effect of a 3% increase in the marginal tax rate.[42]

"Corruption also decreases the returns that a state derives from a given level of investment. When corruption distorts the approval process for an investment project, the rate of return on investment ceases to be a determining factor in the cost-benefit analysis."[43] "This can also reduce the rate of return a state derives from existing infrastructure."[44]

Foreign direct investment, as well as domestic investment in developing countries will only flow if the rule of law provides investors with protection of their rights and their assets. This implies that recipient states must have committed codes and standards as well as an independent judiciary that is free from corruption.

In a paper developed by the Australian delegation and circulated at the Fifteenth Asia-Pacific Economic Cooperation (APEC) Ministerial Meeting in Bangkok October 17-18 2003, it is noted that "foreign investors are increasingly looking for good governance practices, sound policies and strong rule of law when making overseas development assistance or foreign direct investment (FDI) decisions. Returns on investment and aid will boost development".

---

[41] The State and Civil Society in the Fight Against Corruption: Defining the Challenge: 8th International Anti-Corruption Conference

[42] Shang-Jin Wei, *How Taxing is Corruption on International Investors*? (Harvard University, February 1997). (mimeograph).

[43] J. Paul Salembier, *Designing Regulatory Systems: A Template for Regulatory Rule-Making- Part I*; Stature Law Review, Volume 23, Number 3 p. 168.

[44] Tanzi, V. and Davoodi, H. "Roads to Nowhere: How Corruption in Public Investment Hurts Growth", 1988 / 12 *Economic Issues*, IMF.

Over the years there has been much speculation on the factors which are critical for successful economic growth in poor countries. Is the most important factor good economic policy? Or is geography and natural resources the key driver? What about the role that institutions play? How important are factors like political stability, property rights, legal systems, patterns of land tenure, etc? A new paper[45] by William Easterly of the Centre for Global Development and Ross Levine of the University of Minnesota suggests that institutions are by far the most important factor. The authors show that "countries with good institutions tend to do all right with good or bad policies,"[46] and those countries lacking in quality institutions do badly, irrespective of the economic policy environment. Surprisingly, their study concluded that there is no clear connection between incomes and geography – other than the fact that geographic advantages typically lead to a good institutional setting.

I had the experience of living through one example of just this. The forest products company for which I worked for in the early 1990's was interested in examining the feasibility of building a pulp mill in Russia. This was the heyday of glasnost and perestroika of President Gorbachev or openness and restructuring. Given the new open society, more books and newspapers were being published – producing a shortage of paper in the former USSR. We had a joint venture partner in Russia, and another partner in Canada – the latter manufactured pulp mill equipment. The role of our company was twofold; namely to provide mill design assistance, and manufacturing expertise once the mill was operational; and, secondly, to market the pulp into the world markets for hard currency until such time as the debt (denominated in dollars) was substantially repaid.

In co-operation with our joint venture partners, we completed a preliminary feasibility study, but had to abandon the project for a variety of reasons. The foremost reason was the lack of predictability and stability of public policies, and the lack of understanding of basic, sound business practice on the part of the Russians.

They first offered us timber in a location one thousand kilometres from the site of the proposed mill. When we objected and cited this as a deal-

---

[45] Tropics, Germs and Crops: How endowments influence economic development: NBER Working Paper 9106.

[46] *The Economist,* October 5 2002, p. 74.

breaker, magically and mysteriously timber tracts some 300 kilometres distance were identified – still a long way away. When we expressed concern about the health of these forests (many of the trees were decadent i.e. they had some rot in the middle), we were told not to worry, the rot would all be cut out and only the good wood would be shipped to the mill. The fact that there was an economic cost of doing this type of work didn't seem to be of great importance to the Russians!

In the middle of the conduct of our feasibility study, the USSR disintegrated, and Mr. Yeltsin bolted from the Communist Party. Many of the officials with whom we had been dealing at the Soviet level suddenly reappeared as Russian bureaucrats. The rules of the game were constantly changing. Income tax rates, as well as rates of duties on imported machinery were changing by the week.

Our repeated requests for assurances from the highest level of the government for the continuous and guaranteed supplies of wood, energy and chemicals seemed to fall on deaf ears. Who in their right mind would invest US$300 million in a pulp mill without a secure raw material supply? When we posed the question 'to whom should we seek assurances for the supply of raw materials – the U.S.S.R, the Russian Federation or local governments' to Canadian embassy officials in Moscow, they answered 'yes'!

Controlled government prices were disappearing, but no one, including leading economists, could predict where prices were headed. As one can imagine, this played havoc with our financial plans and forecasts.

In many developing countries and emerging economies, joint ventures with local partners are encouraged as the way to do business and at many levels this makes good sense. However, joint ventures with companies or organizations in foreign countries typically create unique challenges. In my business experience with joint ventures in Russia and China, one of the more difficult areas was the consideration of in-kind contributions by foreign partners, and the valuation of these assets. Often, joint venture partners in countries like China and Russia, especially in the 1990's, had very little to bring to the table as their contribution to the joint venture project. In the mid 1990's I was an executive officer with a Canadian company formed by business colleagues of mine at the time, who had a joint venture partner in Shenyang, China. Our mission was to build a medium density fibre board (MDF) mill in China to capitalize on the growth of the middle class in that country and the increasing demand for housing and furniture. MDF is used in the manufacture of furniture and in the production of moulded door skins that are used for doors for houses and garages. The project ultimately came into being – but not as an MDF mill but as a moulded door skin plant (more value-added!). During our initial discussions with our joint venture partner in China, our Chinese partners had very limited access to financial capital and so they offered up in-kind contributions in lieu of cash. These in-kind items consisted of a manufacturing plant (old and outdated) and assorted pieces of equipment (some not relevant to the project at hand!). Our partners proceeded to attempt to have us accept these assets at overvalued prices as a proxy for their equity contribution. Clearly, this was a thorny part of our negotiations and one area where we could not agree. Fortunately, other solutions were found.

In Russia, we encountered similar problems with our joint venture partners in that country. We encountered over valued in-kind contributions together with attempts to include items in the joint venture capital expenditure budget (CAPEX) that were not legitimate project costs. These items included a power grid which would benefit the area generally above and beyond the pulp mill, and items like a school, hospital, and nursery – costs that in Canada would in most instances be covered by the state.

All the Russian players wanted a piece of the hard currency receipts that would be generated by the sale of the pulp in world markets. We actually developed a hard currency cash flow model in addition to the normal versions to ensure that the hard currency was rationed in the best possible way. Even with that, we had to tell the Russians that the vast majority of the pulp would have to be exported outside of Russia for at least 10 years to satisfy the debt holders. This was not exactly what they had originally intended because they wanted to create a more robust domestic supply of paper; however, the Russians realized they had little choice and they reluctantly accepted this reality.

We traveled to what had been a forestry commune, or *lespramholz,* which was an area devoted to forest industry activities. It consisted of pulp mills, sawmills and included residential areas, schools, hospitals and recreational areas for the workers. We were hosted by the director of the operation who provided us with a guided tour of the operations followed by a lavish dinner interspersed with a flurry of toasts with our vodka-filled glasses.

Another example is the experience of George Cohon, the founder of McDonald's Restaurants of Canada. It took him seven years to establish the first McDonald's hamburger outlet in Moscow. To his credit, neither he nor his officials ever entertained discussions about bribes. Perhaps that is why it took so long to bring his project to fruition! His strategy was and is to build a rouble business and to integrate backwards into MacDonald's traditional supply chain. By building a rouble business he created more support in Russia for his enterprise and he waited for the rouble to be convertible and/or to participate in the limited auctions of 'hard currency'. It would appear that his strategy was a successful one.

In Moscow in 1991 it was evident that the Pizza Hut Company took a different approach to their business. A Pizza Hut operation in the centre of town, and not far from the original MacDonald's, consisted of a rouble restaurant and a 'hard currency' version next door – both working from the same kitchen! There was a huge line-up at the rouble restaurant and no line at all at the other. Our group of five was charged about US$150 for a couple of pizzas, 1-2 beers each, apple pie and coffee all around. The high price was explained by the fact that the items listed on the menu were priced in roubles, but were converted to dollars at the official exchange rate – not the black market rate which everyone was using. Considering that we were in Moscow on business and working closely with the Russian authorities, we weren't about to try and argue that the official exchange rate was a questionable one to use.

These examples illustrate how corruption impedes the economic growth of developing countries on two levels. First, it robs the revenue of business owners in developing countries by claiming a portion of their profits through the payment of bribes. In countries such as Indonesia, businesses, especially small ones, are forced by public officials to pay bribes in order for the enterprise to remain in business.[47] In Indonesia

---

[47] Tanzi,584.

there is a term for these payments (pungli). These payments can raise the cost of doing business in some countries by as much as 20 percent of the operating costs. Secondly, the uncertainty of widespread corruption can act as a deterrent for potential investors.[48] Corruption can reduce foreign direct investment because it has the same affect as a tax - the less predictable the level of corruption (the higher is its variance) and the greater its impact on foreign direct investment.[49] A higher variance would have corruption behave like a random tax, thus deterring investors. In fact, IMF Economist Paolo Mauro (1996) finds empirical evidence that corruption lowers economic growth.[50] Using the Business International Indices of corruption, Mauro finds a one deviation improvement in the corruption index causes investment to rise by 5% of the GDP, and the annual growth rate of GDP per capita to rise by half a percentage point.[51]

However, up until the 1997 financial crisis it appeared that some countries in Southeast Asia were growing economically despite their corrupt governments. Developing countries with corrupt practices such as Indonesia, Thailand and Korea were just some of the countries thought to have grown economically while tolerating corrupt practices.[52] It was argued, that in places such as Indonesia where corruption was institutionalized rather than random corruption, the country continued to grow economically. Researchers Leff (1964) and Huntington (1968) argue that the high rates of growth in corrupt countries in South East Asia were possible because corruption in the form of bribery actually enhanced capital flows by removing government red tape that prevented investment.[53]

However, contrary to this belief, although these corrupt countries

---

[48] Paolo Mauro. *The Effects of Corruption on Growth, Investment, and Government Expenditure*. IMF Working Paper 96/98. Washington: International Monetary Fund (1996), 86.

[49] Vito Tanzi. *Corruption Around the World: Causes, Consequence, Scope and Cures*. IMF Staff Papers, Vol.45 , No.4 , International Monetary Fund, (December 1998) p.586.

[50] Paolo, p. 87.

[51] Ibid.

[52] Rose-Ackerman, Susan. *Corruption: A Study of Political Economy*. (New York: New York Academic Press, 1978), 32 Chapter Preview, Institute of International Economics http://www.iie.com/publications/chapters_preview/12/2iie2334.pdf

[53] Tanzi, p. 581.

had satisfactory economic growth, they became susceptible to economic collapse. Eventually corrupt practices feed on themselves and multiply, producing higher illegal pay-offs, until growth is undermined.[54] By tolerating corruption, allowing for instance 5 to 10 percent of the value of public projects to go towards bribes, this may create pressures to increase payoffs to 10 to 15 percent, leading to a self-destructive cycle. Costs from these activities suggest that corruption, despite cutting through bureaucratic 'red tape' actually has a negative impact on the rate of growth of countries. Corruption also distorts the allocation of resources by reducing government expenditure on education, health and infrastructure maintenance. This prevents the advancement of developing countries. Clearly, corruption is not something a country will 'grow out of.' Without significant policy changes to reform this downward cycle, corruption will continue to impede financial flows.

Some argue that corruption is driven by poverty. While I agree that this is somewhat true for low level corruption (e.g. paying a bribe to avoid a speeding ticket or to obtain an import permit, etc.) I believe that 'big ticket' corruption by political and other leaders is motivated rather by greed. I made this point in remarks I made at the Parliamentary Assembly of the Council of Europe during the 2nd Part of the 2006 Ordinary Session in Strasbourg, France April 10th 2006 during the Debate on Poverty and the fight against corruption in the Council of Europe member states.

"I am very pleased to participate in the debate on Poverty and the fight against corruption in the Council of Europe member states and I would like to thank Mr. Alain Cousin, the rapporteur, for his excellent work on this topic. Mr. Cousin's draft resolution deserves the support of this assembly to support parliamentarians around the world who are focused on the negative impacts of corruption - and who are fighting to eliminate corruption or reduce it substantially. This is no small task because corruption has become endemic in many of our societies. No country is immune from corruption.

Transparency International ranks countries each year using their

---

[54] Rose-Ackerman, Susan. *Corruption: A Study of Political Economy.* (New York: New York Academic Press, 1978), 32 Chapter Preview, Institute of International Economics http://www.iie.com/publications/chapters_preview/12/2iie2334.pdf

Corruption Perceptions Index. In 2003, Canada was ranked the 11th least corrupt country on a list prepared by Transparency International out of a group of 133 countries. Bangladesh was ranked the most corrupt country. Many member states of the Council of Europe did not glorify themselves on this list. By way of example, Georgia was 127th. Azerbaijan was 125th. Ukraine was 111th. I could go on. On a more positive note, Finland, Iceland and Denmark were ranked the 3 least corrupt countries on the list of 133 countries.

There have been various attempts to measure the impact of corruption on a country's GDP. Experts in this field have estimated that a one unit increase in bribery or corruption (on a scale of zero to 10) would lower real GDP growth by 0.3 to 1.8 percentage points, or by 1% to 1.3% depending on the methodology used.

Not only does corruption affect economic performance but it also creates income distribution inequities - the very few monopolize a country's income and wealth while the majority are mired in poverty. Political instability is often an outcome.

We know that poverty and corruption are highly correlated. Poor countries are likely to be corrupt. The reverse is also true - corrupt countries are likely to be poor. We need to recognize, however, that it is greed, not poverty, that is the factor which motivates government and corporate leaders to engage in corrupt activities.

Parliamentarians around the world are beginning to turn their attention to the fight against corruption and money laundering. The Global Organization of Parliamentarians Against Corruption, or GOPAC, is such an initiative.

The Global Organization of Parliamentarians Against Corruption (GOPAC) was founded in 2002 at a conference hosted by the Canadian House of Commons and Senate. GOPAC now has over 400 members around the world, organized into regional and national chapters. GOPAC is the umbrella organization to motivate, support, and organize regional chapters around the world - chapters that have been formed in North America, in Asia, in Africa, in the Middle East, in the Caribbean, here in Europe, and in the Newly Independent States. Other Chapters are being formed on a regular basis.

So, parliamentarians are increasingly involving themselves in the fight against bribery, corruption and money laundering.

We better understand the destabilizing influence of bribery and corruption, and the economic costs associated with it. We understand also how corruption and money laundering are connected. The Parliamentary Assembly of the Council of Europe has been a leader in the fight against money laundering. Passage of the draft resolution before this Assembly today will continue this good work by attacking corruption in a similar way.

Parliamentarians can work together to find the solutions to these very difficult problems".

CHAPTER 4

THE DISEASES OF BRIBERY AND CORRUPTION

Corruption is defined by the World Bank as "The abuse of public office for private gain". Transparency International defines it as "...the misuse of public power for private profit."

When corruption reaches into the various levels of government, we encounter the problem of exposing persons or high-ranking officials, who illegally enrich themselves at the expense of the development of their state. In addition to the challenges posed by politically exposed persons caught up in potential money laundering operations (a topic which is discussed later) this is why it is sometimes difficult for legislatures to enact legislation that addresses corruption and money laundering – because parliamentarians may realize that they could be exposing their own wrongful acts by voting for a particular piece of legislation! Corrupt politicians and senior officials will often attempt to launder their ill-gotten gains through banks and other financial intermediaries. A corrupt politician or senior government official is often a key player in the crime of money laundering. These individuals are referred to as 'politically exposed persons' (PEP) and create some unique challenges to financial intermediaries who come across a suspicious transaction where a PEP is involved. Many of these individuals follow a particular pattern of corruption which begins by first moving large amounts of illegal funds to trust accounts.[55] This is followed by the creation of companies to provide a layer of obscurity, as well as

---

[55] *Money Laundering and the Misuse of Trusts.* Bakerplatt: A Specialist Professional Group 18 August 2005. http://www.bakerplatt.com/upload/public/Files/1/Money%20Laundering%20and%20the%20Misuse%20of%20Trusts.pdf.

naming 'Nominee Directors' who contribute nothing to the company, and are used instead, to issue money to the true beneficial owner.[56]

On a smaller scale, politically exposed persons can follow corrupt proceedings in three phases: The first is the *placement* step, which involves putting the funds generated from a crime in to a financial system either directly or indirectly. [57] The second involves *layering*, which involves a complex network of financial services and trusts where multiple transactions are used to eliminate an audit trail.[58] Finally, the *integration* stage in which politically exposed persons take the successfully obscured funds and put them back into the economy as legitimate funds.[59]

The gravity of having politically exposed persons involved in scandals can further cause corruption to bleed into banking institutions, who in some cases aid corrupt leaders. Such was the case of Chilean dictator Augusto Pinochet, who illegally profited from his citizens with the help of Riggs Bank in the United States. Having institutions such as banks turn a blind eye to how some of its wealthiest customers obtain their fortune, allowed for the corrupt dealings of Pinochet to continue, long after his term in office.

Founded in 1836, Riggs Bank was involved in one the America's highest profile investigations involving money laundering.[60] This eventually led to record fines being imposed on the Bank for its unlawful actions and the eventual sale of the bank to PNC Financial Services Group Pittsburgh.[61]

Riggs began its banking relationship with Pinochet in 1979 and lasted until 2004. Throughout Pinochet's alleged crimes against humanity, Riggs helped the tyrant set up two offshore corporations in the Bahamas which allowed him to open corporate accounts in order to provide him with easy

---

[56] Ibid.

[57] *Understanding Money Laundering,* Bakerplatt: A Specialist Professional Group 18 August 2005. http://www.bakerplatt.com/upload/public/Files/1/Understanding%20AML.pdf

[58] Ibid.

[59] Ibid.

[60] *Riggs Bank the Fall of an Institution – A Salutary Lesson for us All?* Bakerplatt: A Specialist Profession Group 18 August 2005 http://www.bakerplatt.com/upload/public/Files/1/art%2027%20riggs%20bank.pdf

[61] Ibid.

access to his money.[62] Despite the fact that Pinochet had international arrest warrants issued for him that ordered all bank accounts be terminated, Riggs continued to open accounts in the name of Pinochet's Bahamian corporations.[63] In December of 2001, media outlets began advertising Riggs' relationship with Pinochet, citing the fact that the bank was holding over $1 million in a bank account for him. Riggs, in response, altered the names on the personal account, deleting any reference to Pinochet in the titled holder of the account and prevented any electronic searching or tracking of his account and finances.[64] After more than two decades of aiding Pinochet's scandals, Riggs decided, in 2002, to close his accounts, sending $6 million directly to Pinochet.[65]

Further to their implication of aiding dictator Pinochet, in 1995 Riggs continued to aid corruption in the developing world by ignoring its obligations under the Anti-money Laundering Laws in its banking institutions in Equatorial Guinea. Riggs managed one of the most corrupt banking institutions in the developing world, allowing suspicious transactions to take place without notifying authorities. This included having the Equatorial Guinea President bring in suitcases of banknotes worth US$13 million without accounting for its origin, and allowing Riggs bank managers to profit over $1 million in oil revenues. The growing scrutiny surrounding the bank's dealings eventually led to Riggs closing all of its Equatorial Guinea accounts in February 2004.

Corruption which is fostered by politically exposed persons has the potential of perpetuating global corruption. With access to vast amounts of profits and with the cooperation of institutions such as Riggs, these individuals are able to evade compliance with anti-money laundering laws.

These incidents are more prevalent in less developed nations. The World Bank, in its World Development Report 2002, states, "Across countries there is evidence that higher levels of corruption are associated with lower growth and lower levels of per capita income".

---

[62] Ibid.
[63] Ibid.
[64] Ibid.
[65] Ibid.

The economic costs associated with bribery and corruption is very real, and at the same time illusive. Transparency International's Global Corruption Report (see next page) estimates that a one unit increase in bribery or corruption (on a scale of zero to 10) would lower real GDP growth by 0.3 to 1.8 percentage points, or by 1% to 1.3% depending on the study and/or methodology.[66]

---

[66] *Transparency International*, Global Corruption Report 2001, Table 1, p. 256.

Table 1: Impact of increasing corruption by one unit [1]

Author(s)	Impact on	Finding
Mauro (1996)	Real per capita GDP growth	−0.3 to −1.8 percentage points
Leite and Weidmann (1999)	Real per capita GDP growth	−0.7 to −1.2 percentage points
Tanzi and Davoodi (2000)	Real per capita GDP growth	−0.6 percentage points
Abed and Davoodi (2000)	Real per capita GDP growth	−1 to −1.3 percentage points
Mauro (1996)	Ratio of investment to GDP	−1 to −2.8 percentage points
Mauro (1998)[2]	Ratio of public education spending to GDP	−0.7 to −0.9 percentage points
Mauro (1998)[3]	Ratio of public health spending to GDP	−0.6 to −1.7 percentage points
Gupta, Davoodi and Alonso-Terme (1998)	Income inequality (Gini coefficient)	+0.9 to +2.1 Gini points
Gupta, Davoodi and Alonso-Terme (1998)	Income growth of the poor	−2 to −10 percentage points
Ghura (1998)	Ratio of tax revenues to GDP	−1 to −2.9 percentage points
Tanzi and Davoodi (2000)[4]	Measures of government revenues to GDP ratio	−0.1 to −4.5 percentage points
Gupta, de Mello and Sharan (2000)[5]	Ratio of military spending to GDP	+1 percentage point
Gupta, Davoodi and Tiongson (2000)[6]	Child mortality rate	+1.1 to 2.7 deaths per 1,000 live births
Gupta, Davoodi and Tiongson (2000)[7]	Primary student dropout rate	+1.4 to 4.8 percentage points
Tanzi and Davoodi (1997)[8]	Ratio of public investment to GDP	+0.5 percentage points
Tanzi and Davoodi (1997)[9]	Per cent of paved roads in good condition	−2.2 to −3.9 percentage points

1. Corruption is measured on a scale of 0 (highly clean) to 10 (highly corrupt).
2. Three other measures of education spending are also reported in this study.
3. Three other measures of health spending are also reported in this study.
4. This study covers 15 types of government revenues.
5. Three additional measures of military spending are also reported in this study.
6. Four additional indicators of health are reported in this study.
7. Four additional indicators of education are reported in this study.

8. *Two additional measures of public spending are also reported in this study.*
9. *Four additional indicators of infrastructure are used in this study.*

Source: Transparency International, Global Corruption Report, page 256

Stable and sound government institutions are more important than good economic policy or geography according to a recent paper released by the Centre for Global Development.[67] The institutions of government to which they refer include political stability, property rights, legal systems, patterns of land tenure and general good governance. In fact, policy and geography don't even come close to the impact of institutions on the rate of growth in poor countries.

In Uganda, it has been estimated that bribes increase a company's costs by 8%.[68] This estimate of 8% was recently mentioned in the context of Kenya by Britain's High Commissioner to Kenya as the cost of corruption in that country as well. This rough estimate of the economic loss that corruption ravages on a domestic economy (8%), therefore, seems to have some credibility and agreement. This figure of 8% relates more to institutionalized bribery and corruption and not directly tied to the 'big-ticket' type of corruption where the country's 'elites' skim off the 'economic cream' and move it into offshore bank accounts. It would seem to me that 8% is a minimum, depending on the country and the leadership at any point in time.

Bribes may also introduce greater health, safety and environmental risks when rules are ignored once money has changed hands. The reason for this is that bribes are often paid to relax rules and regulations that are designed to protect the public. The net result is that a country's citizens are exposed to greater risks while others benefit financially.

Quite clearly, corruption is a disease that affects every functioning aspect of governments. To better understand the correlation between corruption and good governance, researcher Tony Hahn created an Index of Public Governance (IPG). Hahn uses 3 levels of measurement to compute the index, drawing on data from the Freedom House's 2004 indices of

---

[67] 69 *Tropics, Germs and Crops: How endowments influence economic development.* NBER Working paper 9106

[68] *The Economist,* March 2nd 2002, p. 12.

political rights and civil liberties, the Transparency International's Corruptions Perceptions 2004 Index and the Economic Freedom of the Worlds 2004 Annual Report. Each set of data represents a democratic and capitalist perspective of government based on the fundamentals that good governance ensures the ability of citizens to vote, encourages free enterprise, improves quality of life and allows citizens to exercise their civil liberties.

Hahn's Index ranks 114 countries, revealing New Zealand at the top of the list with the highest model of good governance with a ranking of 9.45 our of 10. Following closely behind is Finland, Switzerland, Iceland and Denmark. Also included in the top ten are the United Kingdom with a ranking of 9.2, as well as Australia and Canada, each of which have a perfect score in the areas of political rights and civil liberties. Surprisingly the United States missed the top ten by one, ranking 11th with a score of only 8.2 on economic freedom.

Most importantly however, are the results for Africa. The first of the African countries to make the list is Botswana, which ranks 29th with a score of 7.52, along with Mauritius and South Africa following closely behind. What is interesting about this, as Hahn points out, is that unemployment for Botswana is over 20% and a third of the population is living with HIV/AIDS. Comparing the Index rankings with indicators of development such as life expectancy and literacy, Botswana in comparison to South Africa and Mauritius is gravely behind, with a life expectancy at 33.38 which is less than half the expected age of Mauritians. Another African nation worth noting is war-torn Sierra Leone, which ranks 74th on the Index of Public Governance, ahead of both Russia (91st place) and China (99th place). Yet in comparison to indicators of development, China and Russia also greatly surpass Sierra Leone.

Hahn points to history and culture to explain why a country can have a positive ranking in the Index of Public Governance and a low incidence of development. He argues that if countries that have the foundations of good governance continue with their efforts, development will follow. This means if countries like Sierra Leone stick to the path of comparatively good governance, while countries like Russia do not, than the indicator of development should rise for Sierra Leone in comparison with Russia.

In fact, Hahn's hypothesis on the relationship between corruption and poverty appears to be supported in a correlation analysis between Hahn's IPG and GDP per capita. To undertake this analysis, I conducted a correlation analysis between Hahn's IPG and GDP per capita (2003). The results indicate that there is a correlation between GDP per capita and good governance at the 73% level and when using the GDP per capita on a Purchasing Power Parity[69] basis (2003), an even greater correlation was revealed at the 77% level. (See Table 2)

Table 2: Correlation Coefficient Matrix Corruption and GDP per Capita (2002)

	Index of Public Governance (IPG) (2004)	GDP per Capita (2003)	GDP per Capita (PPP) (2003)
Index of Public Governance (IPG) (2004)	100%	73%	77%
GDP per Capita (2003)	73%	100%	97%
GDP per Capita (PPP) (2003)	77%	97%	100%

Source: World Bank and Hahn's Index of Public Governance

The results of the correlation matrix reveal a positive relationship between GDP per capita and IPG. This means that people in countries with lower GDP per capita are more likely to believe they are not well governed as expressed by factors in Hahn's IPG. Although a correlation analysis does not measure the level of significance, we can conclude from these results that the two variables are highly related.

In fact, results that further support this correlation are the findings

---

[69] Purchasing Power Parity or PPP is a method of measuring the relative purchasing power of different countries' currencies over the same types of goods and services. Because goods and services may cost more in one country than in another, PPP permits more accurate comparisons of standards of living across countries. PPP estimates use price comparisons of comparable items, but since not all items can be matched exactly across countries and times, the estimates are not always "robust."

of a correlation analysis done between the indices of Hahn's Index of Public Governance and GDP per capita. The indices of Hahn's IPG were analyzed to test their individual correlation with GDP per Capita. The four indices consisted of corruption, civil liberties, political rights, and economic freedom. As Table 3 indicates, the highest correlation is between corruption and GDP per Capita and GDP per capita on a PPP basis with 82.0% and 82.3% respectively.

Table 3: Correlation Coefficient Matrix of GDP per Capita and the Four Indices of Hahn's IPG

	GDP per capita (PPP) (2003)	GDP per Capita (2003)	Political Rights	Civil Liberties	Corruption	Economic Freedom
GDP per capita (PPP) (2003)	1	0.966677638	0.560472929	0.649710444	**0.823090946**	0.600506969
GDP per Capita (2003)	0.966677638	1	0.504935767	0.602509822	**0.819641361**	0.553780891
Political Rights	0.560472929	0.504935767	1	0.925404637	0.514066282	0.515668537
Civil Liberties	0.649710444	0.602509822	0.925404637	1	0.631372017	0.539920923
Corruption	**0.823090946**	**0.819641361**	0.514066282	0.631372017	.1	0.499188468
Economic Freedom	0.600506969	0.553780891	0.515668537	0.539920923	0.499188468	1

Source: Statistics Canada. Table prepared by Parliamentary Information and Research Service, Library of Parliament.

In addition to the data in Table 3 which found corruption and GDP per capita to be highly correlated, Table 3 also illustrates that in comparison to political rights, civil liberties and economic freedom, corruption is the most significant indicator of GDP per capita. This is vital for understanding the relationship between economic development and corruption. This evidence of a highly correlated relationship indicates that efforts put into combating corruption will benefit the development of poor countries.

However, good governance is not the only indicator of corruption; - poverty plays a role as well. A book[70] recently published by the IMF includes studies on the impact of corruption on economic performance. Amongst the findings are the following:

- social indicators (e.g. child mortality rate, school drop-out rates) are worse where corruption is high;
- countries with higher corruption tend to have lower per capita income, a higher incidence of poverty and greater income inequality;
- tax revenue is lower in more corrupt countries;
- transition economies that have made more progress on structural reform tend to be less corrupt; and
- decentralization of taxation and spending improves governance.

Is there any empirical evidence linking poverty with corruption? If one compares the top ten most corrupt nations (as measured by the 2003 Corruption Perceptions Index developed by Transparency International) with Gross National Income (GNI) per capita (purchasing power parity method) for the year 2001 (the most recent year available) as disclosed by the World Bank, we find the following in Table 4.

Table 4: Gross National Income for 10 Most Corrupt Nations

10 most corrupt nations* (starting with the worst)	GNI per capita (U.S.A. = $34,280)**	GNI world ranking (out of 208)**
Bangladesh	$1,600	173
Nigeria	$790	199
Haiti	$1,870	166
Paraguay	$5,180	106
Tajikistan	$1,140	184
Georgia	$2,580	148
Cameroon	$1,580	174
Azerbaijan	$2,890	141
Angola	$1,690	171
Kenya	$970	190

*Source: Transparency International: Corruption Perceptions Index 2003

**Source: World Bank: 03 World Bank Atlas (no GNI per capita figure for Myanmar although in top ten of most corrupt nations)

---

[70] George T. Abed and Sanjeev Gupta. (Ed.) *Governance, Corruption, and Economic Performance*, 2002.

With the exception perhaps of Paraguay, the ten most corrupt nations are amongst the poorest nations (all of them in the top 1/3 quartile of poverty).

For a number of developing countries, I compared gross national income per capita for the year 2001, and the level of corruption, as represented by Transparency International's Corruption Perceptions Index (CPI). Transparency International (TI) has published its annual Corruption Perceptions Index (CPI) since 1995. This index has evolved into a leading indicator in social sciences. The goal of the CPI is to provide data on extensive perceptions of corruption within countries. The CPI is a composite index, making use of 17 surveys of businesspeople and assessments by country analysts.

Conducting a correlation analysis between the Transparency International Corruption Perceptions Index (CPI-2003)) and GDP per capita (2002), the results reveals there is a strong correlation between low GDP per capita and corruption. Corruption is highly correlated with both GDP per capita and GDP per capita on a Purchasing Power Parity basis (PPP), at the 86% and 88% level respectively. Countries with higher GDP per capita tend to have a lower perception of the presence of corruption as expressed by the corruption index.

Keeping in mind the difficulties associated with the interpretation of a correlation coefficient between corruption and GDP, I calculated the correlation between corruption as expressed by the CPI (2003) and GDP per capita (2002). The results in Table 5 show that there is a strong correlation between GDP per capita and corruption as reported in many other studies. Corruption is highly correlated with both GDP per capita and GDP per capita on a PPP basis, at the 86% and 88% level respectively (see Table 5).

Table 5: Correlation Coefficient Matrix
Corruption and GDP per Capita (2002)

	Corruption Index	GDP per Capita	GDP per Capita (PPP)
Corruption Index (2003)	100%	**86%**	**88%**
GDP per Capita	86%	100%	95%
GDP per Capita (PPP)	88%	95%	100%

Source: World Bank and Transparency International data 2003

Empirical analysis on corruption is a relatively new domain of research. The research mostly concentrates on cross-country analysis and uses GDP as an indicator or proxy of a country's wealth. Although there is generally a strong correlation between GDP per capita and corruption reported in many studies, there is no general agreement on the existence of a causality link or on the direction of causality between the two variables. The direction of causality between corruption and other economic and social variables can be difficult to measure. Often enough, certain types of government, poor institutions, inequality and lack of competition and poverty may go along with corruption. However, Lambsdorff (2004) warns, "These indicators and corruption are sometimes two sides of the same coin."[71]

Indeed, it can be useful to examine the correlation between corruption and some economic indicators, such as GDP per capita, but it is necessary to avoid drawing ironclad conclusions with respect to causalities.[72]

For example, while corruption possibly lowers GDP per head, poorer countries lack the resources to fight corruption. This simultaneous relationship is hard to disentangle. In fact, Hall and Jones (1999) maintain that there exist many simultaneity problems associated with corruption correlation analysis. One of them is related to the fact that the indicator

---

[71] Johann G. Lambsdorff, *Corruption in Empirical Research – A Review*, International Anti-Corruption Conference, 2004.
[72] Ibid.

of corruption itself is based on perceptions. If countries at an equal stage of development differ in the extent of corruption, perceptions may be informative. But if countries differ widely in their development, perception may be less reliable. A simple regression cannot address this problem. The approach taken by Hall and Jones (1999) and by other researchers in the field is called the instrumental variable technique.[73]

A literature review on the relationship between poverty and corruption reveals the following: From Mauro (1998):

> "Corruption is likely to occur where restrictions and government intervention lead to the presence of excessive profits. Examples include trade restrictions (such as tariffs and import quotas), industrial policies favouring certain sectors (such as subsidies and tax deductions), price controls, multiple exchange rate practices and foreign exchange allocation schemes, and government-controlled provision of credit."
>
> "From economic theory, one would expect corruption to reduce economic growth by lowering incentives to invest (for both domestic and foreign entrepreneurs). In cases where entrepreneurs are asked for bribes before enterprises can be started, or corrupt officials later request shares in the proceeds of their investments, corruption acts as a tax, though one of a particularly pernicious nature, given the need for secrecy and the uncertainty as to whether bribe takers will live up to their part of the bargain. Corruption could also be expected to reduce growth by lowering the quality of public infrastructure and services, decreasing tax revenue, causing talented people to engage in rent-seeking rather than productive activities, and distorting the composition of government expenditure. At the same time, there are some theoretical counterarguments. For example, it has been suggested that government employees who are allowed to exact bribes might work harder and that corruption might help

---

[73] The technique isolates the pure impact of corruption on a variable by using instruments (i.e., another variable) which are correlated with corruption and which have no impact on the studied variable.

entrepreneurs get around bureaucratic impediments."[74]

Lambsdorff (2004) offers a review of empirical efforts that have been made to ascertain the influence of corruption on GDP. His survey shows ambiguous results:

"Keefer and Knack (1995) report that a variable of institutional quality, which incorporates corruption among other factors, exerts a significant negative impact on GDP growth. But Brunetti, Kisunko and Weder (1997) produced insignificant results. Mauro (1995) found a slightly significant impact in a bivariate regression. But as soon as the ratio of investment to GDP was included as an explanatory variable, this impact disappeared. Making use of data on corruption provided by the Political Risk Services Group, Mauro (1997) produced significant results at a 95 per cent confidence level. A significant positive impact is also reported by Leite and Weidmann (1999) and Poirson (1998). On the basis of mixed evidence, it is sometimes argued that corruption primarily impacts on the accumulation of capital, which can be derived from the ratio of investment to GDP, but it does not clearly affect the productivity of capital, because otherwise a link between corruption and growth of GDP should be observable".

"But the question of whether corruption should affect levels of GDP or its growth may be debated. In line with Paldam [1999] and Lambsdorff (1999) argues that lack of corruption is a factor for the production of GDP. If this holds, growth of GDP should not be explained by absolute levels of corruption but by a change in these levels. This is investigated by Lambsdorff (1999) in a cross-section of 53 countries. He uses data by World Economic Forum based on responses to the question of whether corruption has decreased in the past 5 years. This variable is shown to better explain growth of GDP as opposed to absolute levels of corruption."[75]

It is sometimes argued that corruption is a cultural matter. Maybe so, but that excuse does not make it right. It just tells you

---

[74] Paolo Mauro, *Corruption: Causes, Consequence, and Agenda for Further Research*. IMF, 1998.

[75] Lambsdorff (2004).

that it will be more difficult and take more time to route out.

In his novel, *The In-Between World of Vikram Lall*, M.G. Vassanji describes the role Mr. Lall played as a go-between for bribes directed to the corrupt Kenyan President, Jomo Kenyatta (the 'Old Man') and his Ministers in the mid 1960's following the Mau Mau guerrilla war. Although the book is written as fiction, it undoubtedly reflects the way that the government conducted business at that time (and to this day - notwithstanding the departure of President Moi in 2002!). In the book Mr. Lall works directly for one of Kenyatta's Ministers, Paul Nderi. He describes the experience this way:

> "I was doing well in my job with Paul Nderi; the salary was modest, in accordance with government schedules, but the Christmas bonuses from Paul, in thick flabby envelopes, were hugely generous, and I could hardly refuse the car and house allowance he gave me. One day in my absence the two Americans Jim and Gerald left a thick manila envelope full of hard currency at my home as a present for Shobha's birthday and I let her convince me to put the sum aside for a rainy day, just in case. Perhaps I was influenced by my boss Paul Nderi's cold calculations. Once he had uttered an aphorism: If you don't take it, someone else will; but if you take it, my friend, at least you could do someone some good. How right that sounds. Total corruption, I've been told, occurs in inches and proceeds through veils of ambiguity."[76]

He goes on to say:

> "The mouse blows kisses as it nibbles away, was the Javeris' modus operandi. You ate and let others eat, was the more widely quoted adage of the day, to which all our city's business leaders subscribed. Bribes were extorted, offered, paid until they became casual as handshakes. My brother-in-law Chand explained the situation this way, with his businessman's cynical humour and folksy wisdom: Bribes were a form of taxation; before the

---

[76] Vassanji, M.G. , *The In-Between World of Vikram Lall*, (Doubleday Canada, 2003). p. 291.

Europeans arrived, the Africans collected a tax called hongo which you paid if you passed through their area. Missionaries and explorers had all paid hongo in the past, having learned from the Swahili, Ukiwa na udhia, penyeza rupia: when in trouble, offer a dollar. A bribe today was simply hongo tax, payment for services rendered, or for permission to pass on unobstructed to the next stage of your enterprise. Since the government paid so little to its employees, they simply collected their own hongo, calling it 'tea money'. In most of the countries of the world, he claimed, people were used to paying this surcharge. I had been appointed the Javeris' facilitator; I could open doors for them that would otherwise remain shut. My influence reached far, for I had been chosen: I had recourse to the fount of all power in the country. I had the ears of the Old Man..."[77]

These excerpts from the novel say it all about how corruption can creep in and eventually take over, and how it gets rationalized and accepted as the norm.

More and more people, however, see the harmful aspects of corruption and will not tolerate it any longer. There is a growing appetite for stronger action against corruption and related money laundering. These initiatives take time to develop and evolve, however. An example of this took place at the January 2004 Summit of the Americas in Monterrey, Mexico. "U.S. diplomats arrived in Monterrey with a controversial plan to act against countries regarded as corrupt, including barring them from future America's summits."[78] The plan was not approved because of the perceived difficulties in arriving at a set of criteria, which would dictate which countries were corrupt and which were not. The countries represented at the Summit did agree, however, to discuss at future meetings corruption fighting measures. Incremental progress is better than no progress at all!

So-called 'rich' countries are not immune from corruption either. As my former boss and renowned forest economist Mike Apsey rightly points

---

[77] Ibid, p. 333.
[78] Paul Knox, *The Globe & Mail*, January 13, 2004, p. A5.

out in his book, *What's All This Got to do with the Price of 2 X 4s?*,[79] we in the developed economies shouldn't feel 'holier than thou' because we are not immune from corruption ourselves. After the uncovering of the sponsorship scandal in Canada, we also slipped in the worldwide ranking to 12th place (the 12th least corrupt country) on a list of 146 countries. The Government of Canada appointed Mr. Justice John Gomery in 2004 to enquire into the operation of the government's sponsorship program – a program that was abused by bureaucrats, with possibly some political interference, in the attempt to raise the profile of the federal government in the province with separatist tendencies - the Province of Quebec. The mismanagement of the sponsorship program has had severe implications for the federal government and the Liberal Party of Canada. The political fallout has been very pronounced – and rightly so. Advertising contracts of significant amounts were directed to Liberal Party friendly firms (also not by chance these individuals were strong federalists opposed to the separation of Quebec from Canada) who then extracted lucrative and often excessive commissions. Accountability and transparency were non-existent and internal management controls sorely lacking.

The following paragraphs are excerpted from a 2003 statement by Peter Eigen, Chairman of Transparency International:

The Transparency International's Corruption Perceptions Index, released in 2003, and presented on the next pages, points to high levels of corruption in many rich countries as well as poorer ones. Seven out of ten countries score less than 5 out of a clean score of 10 in the TI CPI 2003, which reflects perceived levels of corruption among politicians and public officials in 133 countries. Five out of ten developing countries score less than 3 out of 10, indicating a high level of corruption.

The Transparency International Corruption Perceptions Index ranks 133 countries in terms of the degree to which corruption is perceived to exist among public officials and politicians. It is a composite index, drawing on 17 different polls and surveys from 13 independent institutions carried out among business people and country analysts, including surveys of residents, both local and expatriate.

---

[79] Mike Apsey, *What's All This Got To Do With The Price of 2 x 4's?*, (University of Calgary Press, 2006).

The CPI focuses on corruption in the public sector and defines corruption as the abuse of public office for private gain. The surveys used in compiling the CPI tend to ask questions in line with the misuse of public power for private benefit, with a focus, for example, on bribe-taking by public officials in public procurement. The sources do not distinguish between administrative and political corruption.

Transparency International Corruption Perceptions Index (CPI) 2003

Country rank	Country	CPI 2003 score	Surveys used	Standard deviation	High-low range
1	Finland	9.7	8	0.3	9.2 - 10.0
2	Iceland	9.6	7	0.3	9.2 - 10.0
3	Denmark	9.5	9	0.4	8.8 - 9.9
3	New Zealand	9.5	8	0.2	9.2 - 9.6
5	Singapore	9.4	12	0.1	9.2 - 9.5
6	Sweden	9.3	11	0.2	8.8 - 9.6
7	Netherlands	8.9	9	0.3	8.5 - 9.3
8	Australia	8.8	12	0.9	6.7 - 9.5
8	Norway	8.8	8	0.5	8.0 - 9.3
8	Switzerland	8.8	9	0.8	6.9 - 9.4
11	Canada	8.7	12	0.9	6.5 - 9.4
11	Luxembourg	8.7	6	0.4	8.0 - 9.2
11	United Kingdom	8.7	13	0.5	7.8 - 9.2
14	Austria	8.0	9	0.7	7.3 - 9.3
14	Hong Kong	8.0	11	1.1	5.6 - 9.3
16	Germany	7.7	11	1.2	4.9 - 9.2
17	Belgium	7.6	9	0.9	6.6 - 9.2
18	Ireland	7.5	9	0.7	6.5 - 8.8
18	USA	7.5	13	1.2	4.9 - 9.2
20	Chile	7.4	12	0.9	5.6 - 8.8
21	Israel	7.0	10	1.2	4.7 - 8.1
21	Japan	7.0	13	1.1	5.5 - 8.8
23	France	6.9	12	1.1	4.8 - 9.0
23	Spain	6.9	11	0.8	5.2 - 7.8
25	Portugal	6.6	9	1.2	4.9 - 8.1
26	Oman	6.3	4	0.9	5.5 - 7.3
27	Bahrain	6.1	3	1.1	5.5 - 7.4
27	Cyprus	6.1	3	1.6	4.7 - 7.8
29	Slovenia	5.9	12	1.2	4.7 - 8.8
30	Botswana	5.7	6	0.9	4.7 - 7.3
30	Taiwan	5.7	13	1.0	3.6 - 7.8
32	Qatar	5.6	3	0.1	5.5 - 5.7

33	Estonia	5.5	12	0.6	4.7 - 6.6
	Uruguay	5.5	7	1.1	4.1 - 7.4
35	Italy	5.3	11	1.1	3.3 - 7.3
	Kuwait	5.3	4	1.7	3.3 - 7.4
37	Malaysia	5.2	13	1.1	3.6 - 8.0
	United Arab Emirates	5.2	3	0.5	4.6 - 5.6
39	Tunisia	4.9	6	0.7	3.6 - 5.6
40	Hungary	4.8	13	0.6	4.0 - 5.6
41	Lithuania	4.7	10	1.6	3.0 - 7.7
	Namibia	4.7	6	1.3	3.6 - 6.6
43	Cuba	4.6	3	1.0	3.6 - 5.5
	Jordan	4.6	7	1.1	3.6 - 6.5
	Trinidad and Tobago	4.6	6	1.3	3.4 - 6.9
46	Belize	4.5	3	0.9	3.6 - 5.5
	Saudi Arabia	4.5	4	2.0	2.8 - 7.4
48	Mauritius	4.4	5	0.7	3.6 - 5.5
	South Africa	4.4	12	0.6	3.6 - 5.5
50	Costa Rica	4.3	8	0.7	3.5 - 5.5
	Greece	4.3	9	0.8	3.7 - 5.6
	South Korea	4.3	12	1.0	2.0 - 5.6
53	Belarus	4.2	5	1.8	2.0 - 5.8
54	Brazil	3.9	12	0.5	3.3 - 4.7
	Bulgaria	3.9	10	0.9	2.8 - 5.7
	Czech Republic	3.9	12	0.9	2.6 - 5.6
57	Jamaica	3.8	5	0.4	3.3 - 4.3
	Latvia	3.8	7	0.4	3.4 - 4.7
59	Colombia	3.7	11	0.5	2.7 - 4.4
	Croatia	3.7	8	0.6	2.6 - 4.7
	El Salvador	3.7	7	1.5	2.0 - 6.3
	Peru	3.7	9	0.6	2.7 - 4.9
	Slovakia	3.7	11	0.7	2.9 - 4.7
64	Mexico	3.6	12	0.6	2.4 - 4.9
	Poland	3.6	14	1.1	2.4 - 5.6

66	China	3.4	13	1.0	
	Panama	3.4	7	0.8	2.7 - 5.0
	Sri Lanka	3.4	7	0.7	2.4 - 4.4
	Syria	3.4	4	1.3	2.0 - 5.0
70	Bosnia & Herzegovina	3.3	6	0.7	2.2 - 3.9
	Dominican Republic	3.3	6	0.4	2.7 - 3.8
	Egypt	3.3	9	1.3	1.8 - 5.3
	Ghana	3.3	6	0.9	2.7 - 5.0
	Morocco	3.3	5	1.3	2.4 - 5.5
	Thailand	3.3	13	0.9	1.4 - 4.4
76	Senegal	3.2	6	1.2	2.2 - 5.5
77	Turkey	3.1	14	0.9	1.8 - 5.4
78	Armenia	3.0	5	0.8	2.2 - 4.1
	Iran	3.0	4	1.0	1.5 - 3.6
	Lebanon	3.0	4	0.8	2.1 - 3.6
	Mali	3.0	3	1.8	1.4 - 5.0
	Palestine	3.0	3	1.2	2.0 - 4.3
83	India	2.8	14	0.4	2.1 - 3.6
	Malawi	2.8	4	1.2	2.0 - 4.4
	Romania	2.8	12	1.0	1.6 - 5.0
86	Mozambique	2.7	5	0.7	2.0 - 3.6
	Russia	2.7	16	0.8	1.4 - 4.9
88	Algeria	2.6	4	0.5	2.0 - 3.0
	Madagascar	2.6	3	1.8	1.2 - 4.7
	Nicaragua	2.6	7	0.5	2.0 - 3.3
	Yemen	2.6	4	0.7	2.0 - 3.4
92	Albania	2.5	5	0.6	1.9 - 3.2
	Argentina	2.5	12	0.5	1.6 - 3.2
	Ethiopia	2.5	5	0.8	1.5 - 3.6
	Gambia	2.5	4	0.9	1.5 - 3.6
	Pakistan	2.5	7	0.9	1.5 - 3.9
	Philippines	2.5	12	0.5	1.6 - 3.6
	Tanzania	2.5	6	0.6	2.0 - 3.3
	Zambia	2.5	5	0.6	2.0 - 3.3

100	Guatemala	2.4	8	0.6	1.5 - 3.4
	Kazakhstan	2.4	7	0.9	1.6 - 3.8
	Moldova	2.4	5	0.8	1.6 - 3.6
	Uzbekistan	2.4	6	0.5	2.0 - 3.3
	Venezuela	2.4	12	0.5	1.4 - 3.1
	Vietnam	2.4	8	0.8	1.4 - 3.6
106	Bolivia	2.3	6	0.4	1.9 - 2.9
	Honduras	2.3	7	0.6	1.4 - 3.3
	Macedonia	2.3	5	0.3	2.0 - 2.7
	Serbia & Montenegro	2.3	5	0.5	2.0 - 3.2
	Sudan	2.3	4	0.3	2.0 - 2.7
	Ukraine	2.3	10	0.6	1.6 - 3.8
	Zimbabwe	2.3	7	0.3	2.0 - 2.7
113	Congo, Republic of the	2.2	3	0.5	2.0 - 2.8
	Ecuador	2.2	8	0.3	1.8 - 2.6
	Iraq	2.2	3	1.1	1.2 - 3.4
	Sierra Leone	2.2	3	0.5	2.0 - 2.8
	Uganda	2.2	6	0.7	1.8 - 3.5
118	Cote d'Ivoire	2.1	5	0.5	1.5 - 2.7
	Kyrgyzstan	2.1	5	0.4	1.6 - 2.7
	Libya	2.1	3	0.5	1.7 - 2.7
	Papua New Guinea	2.1	3	0.6	1.5 - 2.7
122	Indonesia	1.9	13	0.5	0.7 - 2.9
	Kenya	1.9	7	0.3	1.5 - 2.4
124	Angola	1.8	3	0.3	1.4 - 2.0
	Azerbaijan	1.8	7	0.3	1.4 - 2.3
	Cameroon	1.8	5	0.2	1.4 - 2.0
	Georgia	1.8	6	0.7	0.9 - 2.8
	Tajikistan	1.8	3	0.3	1.5 - 2.0
129	Myanmar	1.6	3	0.3	1.4 - 2.0
	Paraguay	1.6	6	0.3	1.2 - 2.0
131	Haiti	1.5	5	0.6	0.7 - 2.3
132	Nigeria	1.4	9	0.4	0.9 - 2.0
133	Bangladesh	1.3	8	0.7	0.3 - 2.2

Source: Transparency International

Explanatory notes

A more detailed description of the CPI 2003 methodology is available at http://www.transparency.org/cpi/index.html#cpi *or at* http://www.gwdg.de/~uwv

A CPI 2003 Score relates to perceptions of the degree of corruption as seen by business people, academics and risk analysts, and ranges between 10 (highly clean) and 0 (highly corrupt).

A Surveys Used refers to the number of surveys that assessed a country's performance. A total of 17 surveys were used from 13 independent institutions, and at least three surveys were required for a country to be included in the CPI.

Standard Deviation indicates differences in the values of the sources: the greater the standard deviation, the greater the differences of perceptions of a country among the sources.

High-Low Range provides the highest and lowest values of the different sources.

Corruption is perceived to be pervasive in Bangladesh, Nigeria, Haiti, Paraguay, Myanmar, Tajikistan, Georgia, Cameroon, Azerbaijan, Angola, Kenya, and Indonesia, countries with a score of less than 2 in the index. Countries with a score of higher than 9, with very low levels of perceived corruption, are rich countries, namely Finland, Iceland, Denmark, New Zealand, Singapore and Sweden. Some changes can be identified in the CPI. On the basis of data from sources that have been consistently used for the index, improvements can be observed for Austria, Belgium, Colombia, France, Germany, Ireland, Malaysia, Norway, and Tunisia. Noteworthy examples of a worsening situation are Argentina, Belarus, Chile, Canada, Israel, Luxembourg, Poland, USA, and Zimbabwe. Nine out of ten developing countries score less than 5 against a clean score of 10 in the TI CPI 2003.[80]

The chaos in Zimbabwe is a result of the corruption and mismanagement in that country under the leadership (or lack thereof) of Robert Mugabe. In addition to crop failures and shortages in a country that was once the 'breadbasket' of Africa, it was reported more recently that "More than half of the residents in Zimbabwe's capital are either chronically short of water or without any, just days before the start of the hottest month of the year. Hardest hit are the poorest residents, many of whom now also have to endure raw sewage running past their homes in what was once one of Africa's most orderly cities."[81]

We must accept that bribery and corruption are pervasive. They occur in many, if not all countries in the world in varying degrees. Some personally encountered cases-in-point follow.

When I worked with a major international accounting firm in Johannesburg in the mid 1970's, these 'cultural' differences became very apparent when I had the occasion to examine the audited financial statements of a company in Mozambique. Located on the balance sheet was an amount in escudos captioned as a 'deferred expenses – representation costs.' Upon further enquiry from the company's auditors, who had given a 'clean' or unqualified report on the financial statements of the company, I discovered that these amounts represented outlays or bribes paid to various public officials over a period of time. They had been capitalized as an asset of the company on the rationale that they represented an enduring and lasting future benefit for the company. They probably did! Needless to say we wrote off these assets on the consolidated financial statements of their parent company in Johannesburg.

This same holding company had previously gone through some incredible gymnastics to obtain a dividend from their wholly owned subsidiary in Mozambique. A bit of history first. In 1974, the Portuguese Government was overthrown by Samora Machel and the Mozambique Liberation Front (Frelimo). The left-wing government nationalized almost

---

[80] Peter Eigen, Chairman, Transparency International, statement at the Foreign Press Association, London, 7 October 2003.

[81] *The Globe and Mail*, Peta Thornycroft (The Daily Telegraph) September 29, 2004, p. A-13.

everything, save the clothes that people were wearing. The most stringent foreign exchange controls were implemented. Remitting dividends to non-resident shareholders outside of Mozambique became a nightmare. To some, however, a problem is simply a solution waiting to be found. The holding company, through its control of the Board of Directors of the company in Mozambique, declared a dividend in escudos, which they promptly exchanged for South African rand on the black market. A private aircraft, which had landed on a landing strip at a remote location in Mozambique, soon collected the individual with a briefcase full of South African rand, and flew the dividend back to Johannesburg and into the hands of the chief financial officer of the holding company! Lo and behold, funds had been repatriated against all odds (and against all the laws of Mozambique). This transaction presented the auditors in Johannesburg with somewhat of an ethical dilemma – but only for a short time. The moral of the story – truth and justice can be relative concepts.

World Corruption at a Glance

Hypocrisy can often go hand-in-hand with corruption. Daniel arap Moi, President of Kenya from 1978 until 2003 and a known corrupt leader, often spoke out in public about the need to fight corruption, at the same time as he raped and pillaged the economy of Kenya. According to the 1999 Transparency International Corruption Perceptions Index, Kenya was in the top ten corrupt countries (or more correctly the bottom ten) as perceived by business people, risk analysts and the general public. Kenya scored 2 out of a possible 10 points, with zero being the most corrupt score.[82] The coffee and tea crops in that country, once the country's economic mainstay, are in a state of disarray and decline – a product of corrupt leaders skimming off the profits. President Moi also argued that western countries should 'back off' and allow Kenyans to deal with corruption in their own way. Fine, perhaps, except that the Government of Kenya seeks the support of the World Bank and the International Monetary Fund at the same time. All of this occurs against a backdrop of growing poverty in Kenya, and a serious decline in the state of the country's infrastructure.

Officials in Kenya are trying to retrieve the funds stolen by President

---

[82] *Transparency International*, 1999 Corruption Perceptions Index.

Moi and his cronies during his twenty-four year rule. "The money was stolen by making fictitious payments on the foreign debt and looting the Central Bank, by demanding kickbacks and obtaining phoney contracts. About $2 billion to $3 billion of the money might still be traceable, say officials involved in the investigation. The higher figure equals roughly a third of Kenya's annual economic output, or half its foreign debt..."[83]

Daniel arap Moi was replaced by Mwai Kibaki who ran on an antigraft campaign platform, in an election in Kenya in 2002. Mr. Kibaki got off to a good start, by firing a large number of judges who were accepting bribes to have charges quashed or dismissed, but then the rot set in again. Mr. Edward Clay, Britain's High Commissioner to Kenya, took the unprecedented step of blasting Mwai Kibaki for not tackling corruption and for the "gigantic looting spree" that followed the 2002 election. He went on to say to an audience in Nairobi in July 2004 that "It is outrageous to think that corruption accounts...for about 8% of Kenya's (gross domestic product). (Mr. Clay) alleged that since Mr. Kibaki's shaky alliance of opposition parties swept to power, the government has been involved in corrupt deals worth about US$250 million."[84]

Does the story in Kenya remind you of the lunatic antics of Robert Mugabe in Zimbabwe? The parallels are obvious and real. The story of Zambia is not much different.

A large mining company in Canada, in the mid 1990's, was anxious to participate in Zambia's copper mine privatization initiative. An agreement-in-principle was negotiated between the company and the Zambian Government, and a representative of the company dispatched to Lusaka to cement the deal and finalize the agreement. One year later, this same individual had packed his bags and relocated with the same company to South America to pursue other business opportunities. The problem? Too much graft being demanded by government leaders and officials at every turn and at every opportunity!

Some years later I recall meeting a parliamentarian from Zambia and I broached the topic of the failed opportunity to attract Canadian investment to Zambia – with the loss in jobs and economic activity. The

---

[83] Peter Goodspeed, *The National Post*, December 18, 2003, p. A-1
[84] *National Post*, (Agence France-Press), July 15 2004.

Zambian MP had co-incidentally followed this story quite closely. Upon digesting what I had said to him, he paused for a long time, then looked me in the eye and said, "My sense was our Minister of Mines became too personally involved in this file"! He didn't need to spell it out for me. What he said was code for "The Minister of Mines, and perhaps others, were hoping to extract large sums to top-up their Swiss bank accounts, in exchange for the satisfactory conclusion of the privatization agreement". Another opportunity was squandered because of the greed of a few.

Nigeria is another case in point. Samuel Ladoke Akintola ruled in Nigeria from 1955-1959.[85] Ryszard Kapuscinski, in his book, *The Shadow of the Sun*, describes him this way: "Akintola was fifty years old, a heavyset man with a wide, baroquely tattooed face. In the past several months he had not left his residence, which was under heavy police guard – he was afraid. Five years ago he had been a middle-class lawyer. After a year of premiership, he already had millions. He simply poured money from the government accounts into his private ones. Wherever you go in Nigeria, you come across his houses – in Lagos, in Ibadan, in Abeokuta. He had twelve limousines, largely unused, but he liked to look at them from his balcony. His ministers also grew rich quickly. We are here in a realm of absolutely fantastical fortunes, all made in politics, or, more precisely, through political gangsterism – by breaking up parties, falsifying election results, killing opponents, firing into angry crowds. One must see this wealth against the background of desperate poverty, in the context of the country over which Akintola ruled - burned, desolate, awash in blood."[86]

Doing business in Indonesia requires a special appreciation of the art of bribery and corruption. Getting deals done in that country often requires that a percentage of revenues or profits find their way into a numbered bank account of an Indonesian general or public official. During the period of President Suharto's rule, I was troubled to learn that a client of mine was obliged to dedicate a portion of the revenues in this way, from the production of crude oil through a joint venture with an Indonesian

---

[85] Taiwo Akinola, *Awolowo/Akintola: The Tango Between Vision and Compromise*, *DAWODU.COM:* Dedicated to Nigeria's Socio-Political issues April 28 2004 <http://www.dawodu.com/awolowo3.htm>.

[86] Ryszard Kapuscinski, *The Shadow of the Sun* (New York: Knopf Canada, 2001). p. 106.

state-owned corporation, Pertamina, totalling millions of US dollars each year.

In a 2004 report of Transparency International[87] the ten most corrupt leaders of the past twenty years were identified, together with an estimate of the amounts that they embezzled. Table 6 documents the shameful list.

Table 6: Transparency International's Report of the Ten most Corrupt Leaders

Despot	Country	Estimate of amount embezzled
President Suharto '67-'98	Indonesia	$15billion - $35 billion
Ferdinand Marcos '72-'86	Philippines	$5 billion - $10 billion
Mobuto Sese Seko '65-'97	Zaire	$5 billion
Sani Abacha '93-'98	Nigeria	$5 billion
Slobodan Milosevic ('89-2000)	Yugoslavia	$1 billion
J-C Duvalier '71-'86	Haiti	$300 - $800 million
Alberto Fujimori '90-2000	Peru	$600 million
Pavlo Lazarenko '96 – '97	Ukraine	$114 - $200 million
Arnoldo Aleman '97 – '2002	Nicaragua	$100 million
Joseph Estrada '98 – 2001	Philippines	$78 - $80 million

Source: Transparency International 2004 Report

The Philippines have two corrupt leaders in the top ten! Quite a record. And how about Pavlo Lazarenko of the Ukraine, taking just one year to salt away $114 to $200 million! He certainly knew what he was doing. Not a long learning curve for him!

If you total these amounts that were stolen from the citizens of these countries (and this list only begins to scratch the surface) one arrives at the grotesque figure of a low of $32 billion to a high of $58 billion from these ten criminals alone. Imagine how many hospitals this could build, or how many schools, or how much food could have been purchased to alleviate hunger and starvation around the globe.

For some reason President Daniel arap Moi didn't make this top ten list, although it is estimated that he and his cronies siphoned off $3 - $4

---

[87] Transparency International, *The Global Corruption Report 2004*.

billion. This amount of money would be "…..enough to provide every child in the country with a free education for the next decade."![88] There is no better example of the squandering of a nation's resources than that of Kenya. "….Kenya, ……in the 19060s and 1970s enjoyed an annual growth rate of about 6.5%. By the end of the rule of Daniel arap Moi, who was elected on an anti-corruption platform, Kenya's economy had stalled and the country was mired in graft. The election of Mwai Kibaki in December, 2002, brought new optimism. Within six months, an anti-corruption act and a public officer ethics act had been passed."[89] Hopefully, for the citizens of Kenya, and for other nations around the world who are monitoring this situation, a lasting solution to corruption in Kenya will be found.

Authorities in the United States estimate that Saddam Hussein accumulated as much as $40 billion during his years in power – funds that he hid in banks in Switzerland, Japan, Germany and other countries!

Kim Jong-il, North Korea's ruler, dictator and 'great leader', is well known for his corrupt practices. "For years he has been using forced labour to mine gold from a mountain in Korea; the gold is deposited directly into his Swiss bank accounts. He has quietly salted away more than $4 billion in those accounts, according to Chuck Downs, an expert on Korea in the Clinton administration. The 'Great Leader' maintains a villa in Geneva (where his son was educated) as well as five other villas in Europe, one in Russia and one in China."[90] All of this is occurring as the economy of North Korea has collapsed, and famine in the hundreds of thousands is evident. In 1998 he ordered 200 Mercedes Benz and paid US$20 million for them, an amount equal to one-fifth of the aid promised to North Korea that year by the United Nations.

Just before Yasser Arafat's death the National Post raised the following issue – "With Yasser Arafat reportedly on his deathbed, many in the Middle East are beginning to pose a delicate question: Where is the money?"[91] It is estimated that Yasser Arafat 'squirreled away' about US$

---

[88] Peter Goodspeed, *National Post*, December 18, 2003, p. A-1.
[89] *National Post*, Peter Eigen, Chairman Transparency International.
[90] *Toronto Star*, January 19, 2003, p. B5 (excerpted from Newsweek Magazine).
[91] *National Post*, November 9, 2004, p. 1.

1 billion into various offshore bank accounts. "Tales of the Palestinian leader's corruption are legendary. In *Arafat's War*, Efraim Karsh wrote that during the 1982 Israeli invasion of Lebanon, Kuwait donated 10 Mercedes ambulances, worth US$600,000, to the Palestine Liberation Organization. Rather than use the ambulances to aid casualties, Arafat sold them at half price to the Syrians, then pocketed the difference."[92]

However, corruption does not only plague governments of the developing world, it can seep in to the most respected and 'legitimate' institutions such as the United Nations. The UN's controversial Oil for Food Programme is under investigation, as members of the UN and programme advisors have been accused of profiting from the programme.

Led by UN Secretary General Kofi Annan, allegations of Annan's involvement and his knowledge of the illegal transactions are under investigation. Further to this, Annan's son may also be implicated because he was working for a Swiss company that is under investigation for abusing the programme.[93] Although no convictions have been made against Annan, his failure to detect or stop the abuses of UN advisors and vendors, weakens the creditability of the UN and proves no institution is immune to corruption.

The tangled web of corruption, bribery and money laundering began in 1996 when the Oil for Food Programme was created in response to the abject poverty of the Iraqi civilians - a combined result from the corrupt dictatorship of Saddam Hussein and the sanctions placed by the UN on Iraq. Following the Iraqi invasion of Kuwait, the sanctions barred UN member states from trading with Iraq in an effort to force the country to disarm.[94] In order to prevent severe suffering to ordinary Iraqis, the UN created the Oil for Food Programme which allowed the Iraqi government to sell small quantities of oil on the world market in exchange for basic

---

[92] Ibid, p. A12.

[93] Holman, Kwame. *The Oil for Food Scandal*. PBS: Online News Hour 17 August 2004. < http://www.pbs.org/newshour/bb/middle_east/july-dec04/oil-for-food_12-3.html>

[94] Phil Hirschkorn and Liz Neisloss. *Oil for food probe names two suspects*. CNN.com 17 August 2004. < http://www.cnn.com/2005/WORLD/meast/08/08/oil.food/>.

necessities such as food, medicine, etc.[95]

According to the Independent Inquiry in to the Oil for Food Programme, money from some of the sales and transactions of the programme never reached the hands of the poor Iraqi citizens. One of the most detrimental allegations is against former Executive Director of the program Benon Sevan, who has been accused of obtaining more than $147 000 in kickbacks.[96] The Independent Inquiry Committee looked into the UN Oil for Food Programme led by Paul Volcker, revealed Sevan benefited from the Programme through the sale of oil allocated by Iraq and had knowledge that some of the oil was purchased by paying an illegal surcharge to Iraq which was in violation of the United Nations rules of the Programme.[97]

Although Sevan denies all allegations, Alexander Yakovlev, a former senior contracts officer for the programme has admitted to the corrupt dealings of the UN.[98] Yakovlev has pled guilty to money laundering and accepting bribes from UN vendors.[99] The Independent Inquiry has found that more than $1.3 million was wired into an account for a dummy firm called Moxyco that Yakovlev established in 2000 in the island of Antigua.[100]

As we await the final results of the Independent Inquiry, the known levels of corruption already revealed are damaging to the reputation of the UN and will require severe internal modifications to prevent fraudulent activity in the future.

On a visit to Rio de Janeiro, Brazil, some years ago, a professional colleague advised me that most large companies had full time 'expediters' on staff. Their role was exclusively to clear the path, by bribing public officials, through the government bureaucracy for export permits, work permits, import permits and a myriad of other necessary approvals

---

[95] Ibid.

[96] Ibid.

[97] Press Release August 8 2005. *Independent Inquiry Committee in to the UN Oil for Food Programme* 17 August 2004. <http://www.iic-offp.org/>.

[98] Ibid.

[99] Ibid.

[100] Phil Hirschkorn and Liz Neisloss. *Oil for food probe names two suspects*. CNN.com 17 August 2004. < http://www.cnn.com/2005/WORLD/meast/08/08/oil.food/>.

essential when doing business in that country. Imagine the economic cost of such an infrastructure and non-productive time-consuming processes.

The stories of corruption are many and varied – the Marcos family in the Philippines, whose wealth at their nadir was estimated by the CIA to be $35 billion; Pinochet in Chile. In India, politicians are paid a modest salary, but they all live a life of opulence. My constituency, which has a large South Asian population, is home to many Indian restaurants and food shops. One day, I ventured into one of them, as I often do, to purchase some samosas and nan bread. The owner of the shop recognized me as the local Member of Parliament. "Aren't you the local M.P.?", he asked. We shook hands and introduced ourselves. "I am amazed that you would come into my shop", he remarked. "Why so?" I responded – puzzled by his comment. "In India," he said, "a member of parliament would probably not enter such modest premises; but, if they did, it would undoubtedly be with 2-3 bodyguards!" I guess if you live by graft and corruption, you make friends and enemies and you need protection from the latter.

So often we see one dictator replaced by another – with very little improvement, or less security and well being, for the average citizen. I recall my experience of attending a meeting of the Immigration and Refugee Appeal Board (IRB) in Toronto. To be a 'fly on the wall' I needed the approval of the IRB, and the lawyers on both sides, which in this case was the lawyer for the appellant arguing against his client's deportation, and the federal government lawyer, arguing the opposite.

The individual in question (let's call him Mr. Ahmed) was from Ethiopia. His lawyer argued that he should be granted refugee status because returning to Ethiopia would put him at grave risk including the possibility of execution by government authorities in that country. On the other hand, the federal government lawyer argued that, notwithstanding such risk, he should be deported anyway because he himself, prior to leaving Ethiopia, had been involved in tyrannical acts and crimes against humanity in his home country. Under Canadian, and perhaps international law, such a case can be made and a refugee claim quashed in circumstances like this.

Mr. Ahmed acknowledged that during the rule of known dictator and despot Halie Selassie he had worked in a political, non-violent way (according to him), as part of a group intent on the overthrow of President Selassie. He was a banker at that time. When President Selassie was finally replaced by Mengistu, Mr. Ahmed, (according to his submissions), was asked to join President Mengistu's secret police – in the accounting department! Mengistu was overthrown himself in 1991. Suddenly all those involved with Mengistu's regime, which turned out to be even more violent and brutal than the Selassie regime, had worked in the accounting department. Federal government lawyers successfully challenged his credibility and he was deported back to Ethiopia – to an uncertain fate. One tyrant replaced by another. Does this sound familiar?

Once, when vacationing in Mexico our guide told me something that certainly didn't surprise me - that in Mexico police officers are uneducated and paid very little, They live on bribes; in fact, the majority of them don't read or write, so how could they be expected to write tickets and arrest reports? The guide also made the point that this seems to be the way that the politicians like things to be; i.e. keep them ignorant and silent!

For politicians in Mexico, when it comes to dealing with the drug lords, the choices are very clear - take the money and run and turn a blind eye; or have you and your family face the consequences of violence turned against you.

Many individuals with idealistic notions of fighting corruption get caught up in the endless cycle of corruption once they are elected. Many of them quickly forget the very reason they sought public office and reinforce the old adage – if you can't fight them, join them!

Corruption has a supply and a demand side

Those who offer or give bribes are just as much the problem as the takers of bribes. The OECD recognized this and in 1997 introduced the Convention on Combating Bribery of Foreign Officials in International Business Transactions. The following year, the Corruption of Foreign Public Officials Act was passed in Canada prohibiting Canadians from bribing foreign officials in the course of doing business (domestic officials excluded!).

Bribery and corruption has both a demand and a supply side. It is therefore important for businesses to refuse to offer bribes. In this regard, the Canadian business community adopted an International Code of

Ethics for Canadian business, which contains, amongst other things, a commitment to the following values – to human rights and social justice; to wealth maximization for all stakeholders; to the operation of a free market economy; and, to a business environment that mitigates against bribery and corruption.

Notwithstanding this code of ethics, a Canadian engineering multinational company, Acres International, was convicted of bribery in connection with a $12 billion mega water project in the African country of Lesotho.

The 1997 OECD Convention on Bribery, now signed by 35 countries states that "enterprises should not, directly or indirectly, offer, promise, give or demand a bribe or other undue advantage to obtain or retain business." The Parliament of Canada implemented its commitment to this OECD Convention in 1999.

Transparency International publishes a Bribe Payers Index, which ranks countries according to their perceived levels of bribery on a scale of zero to 10 (0 representing very high levels of bribery and 10 negligible levels) as perceived by exporters. In its 1999 report, Sweden, Australia and Canada received scores of eight or better, while Malaysia, Italy, Taiwan, South Korea and China scored less than four.[101]

In the war against drugs we often hear about the need to focus on the supply side or the demand side, or vice-versa – or, that we need to attack both ends. Well, bribes are not unlike a habit-forming narcotic. Power does corrupt, and as we have heard, absolute power corrupts absolutely! Indeed, in the fight against corruption, we must address those who would pay bribes and those who would accept them.

How do we deal with the suppliers of bribes?

A 1997 OECD Convention on Bribery, now signed by 35 countries, states that "enterprises should not, directly or indirectly, offer, promise, give or demand a bribe or other undue advantage to obtain or retain business."

The Foreign Corrupt Practices Act in the USA, which was passed in 1977, outlaws the payment of bribes by American firms to foreign officials, political parties, party officials and candidates. At the rate of

---

[101] Transparency International, 1999 Bribe Payers Index.

less than two prosecutions per year on average since the law was passed, one has to question how effective this legislation is.

Most developed countries, but surprisingly not all, have policies in place that preclude the deduction of bribes for purposes of calculating income for taxation purposes!

There are other initiatives designed to make payments from corporations to governments more transparent. One such effort is the *Publish What You Pay* Campaign – a coalition of over 200 NGO's worldwide which is calling for the mandatory disclosure of the payments made by oil, gas and mining companies to all governments to extract natural resources. This campaign was launched by George Soros and founded by Global Witness, Open Society Institute, Oxfam, Save the Children UK, and Transparency International UK.

Another drive has been organized by the *Extractive Industries Transparency Initiative* whose objective is to "increase transparency over payments and revenues in the extractives sector in countries heavily dependent on these resources."

While the objectives of these two initiatives are laudable, it is hard to imagine what positive results they can practically achieve. Amounts paid to developing countries for royalties and resource rents are one thing. Such disclosures might be more readily forthcoming and useful. But what would motivate corporations or individuals to disclose amounts they have paid to governments, government officials or elected individuals in the form of bribes or 'facilitation fees'? What would likewise motivate government officials or elected individuals to disclose these same payments? I have witnessed first hand the negative reaction from the leader of a corrupt nation to this proposition! Corporate leaders will react the same way if they are involved in bribes and corruption. What do they have to gain by disclosing amounts they have paid in bribes?

In 2007, on behalf of the Global Organization of Parliamentarians Against Corruption (GOPAC), I met with the International Public Sector Accounting Standards Board at their meeting in Montreal and asked them to demand more transparency of natural resource revenues in the public accounts of nations and sub-national governments. If acted upon, this would better hold governments to account for these sizeable revenues.

CHAPTER 5

GOOD CORPORATE GOVERNANCE AND THE ROLE OF EDUCATION AND INNOVATION

The Relevance of Good Corporate Governance

What is corporate governance? Milton Friedman, economist and Nobel laureate, provided one of the earliest definitions of corporate governance. "According to Friedman, corporate governance is: '...to conduct the business in accordance with owner or shareholder desires, which generally will be to make as much money as possible, while conforming to the basic rules of the society embodied in law and local customs'. The Toronto Stock Exchange defines corporate governance as '...the process and structure used to direct and manage the business and affairs of the corporation with the objective of enhancing shareholder value, which includes ensuring the financial viability of the business.' In short, corporate governance is more than just improving financial performance. It provides a sound system of checks and balances to supervise senior management *and* fosters a culture of transparency and trust between the primary corporate players and investors."[102]

Too often we learn that corporate managers, in their desire to inflate corporate profits, bend accounting rules or commit outright fraud. One could describe this type of behavior as corporate corruption and it is just as offensive as corruption in the public sector.

Often, members of the boards of directors of corporations are not

---

[102] Unpublished report, September 2003: Corporate Governance in Canada: The Role of the Federal Government. Committee Caucus chaired by Roy Cullen, M.P.

independent of management and not provided with the information they need to challenge management. As John Kenneth Galbraith asserts in his book *The Economics of Innocent Fraud*, "This fraud has accepted ceremonial aspects: One is a board of directors selected by management, fully subordinate to management but heard as the voice of the shareholders. It includes men and the necessary presence of one or two women who need only a passing knowledge of the enterprise; with rare exceptions, they are reliably acquiescent. Given a fee and some food, the directors are routinely informed by management on what has been decided or is already known. Approval is assumed, including for management compensation – compensation set by management itself."[103]

We have all witnessed rising executive compensation (often at ridiculously high levels) during periods of declining corporate profits and/or falling stock market prices. Golden parachutes in the millions of dollars are typically available to 'down-sized' executives concurrent with much 'stingier' packages for other managers and workers.

The former chairman of the US Federal Reserve, Paul Volker, rightly points a finger at the legal and accounting professions who have not been assertive enough, and whose principles have been subordinated to the will of investment bankers and senior management.

I know from personal experience how auditors can be subjected to the wrath of management. As a young chartered accountant working as an audit manager with one of the largest international accounting and auditing firms, I was asked by the audit partner to give approval to the accounting treatment of certain assets which I believed were not in accordance with generally accepted accounting principles. I sought the advice of the firm's technical group at head office and they were in agreement with my interpretation. The transaction involved the question as to whether or not the unrealized gain arising from the translation of monetary assets from US dollars to Canadian dollars at the date of the balance sheet should be included in the profits of the company for the year. The rules seemed clear to me. Conversion gains associated with monetary assets (liquid assets) were to be taken into income for the year and not treated as a deferred

---

[103] John Kenneth Galbraith, *The Economics of Innocent Fraud* (Houghton Mifflin Company, 2004), p. 27.

credit on the balance sheet. The company in question was listed on a stock exchange and the foreign exchange gain was significant (i.e. material in relation to the company's income). The company's management was very reluctant to include the unrealized gain in income for the year because of upcoming labour negotiations. I felt that these considerations were irrelevant – our role as auditors was to assess whether or not the assets and liabilities and income for the year presented fairly the financial position of the company, in accordance with generally accepted accounting principles (GAAP). In the end, I included a note in the audit working papers that presented my arguments, but the audit partner overruled me. Pressure was exerted on me not to include my remarks in writing in the file – but I refused. The company was a significant accounting, tax and management-consulting client of the firm and I felt that our professional judgment had been compromised. It was not long after that when I departed the firm.

Corporate greed and malfeasance reinforce a culture of corruption and add to the challenge of eliminating corruption in both the private and public sectors.

The Role of Education and Innovation

First let us examine the role of parliamentarians in this important area.

The institution of Parliament has a key role to play in fighting corruption. Parliamentarians can hold the executive branch of government to account for their spending and administrative actions. This important role can be achieved in a number of different ways:

- Through debates and questions in the legislature itself;
- Through the work of an auditor general, or accounts chamber, that reports directly to parliament; and,
- By enquiry and investigative work by a public accounts committee of parliament.

At a Commonwealth Parliamentary Association Workshop held in Nairobi, Kenya in December 2001 on the topic *Parliamentary Oversight of Finance and the Budgetary Process* which I attended, a general consensus was reached around the following points:

- Budget plans should be responsive to the priorities of citizens;
- The budget must have the approval of parliament;
- After the passing of the budget, funds expended must be accounted for to avoid the misuse of funds; and
- Mechanisms in place to deter the misuse of funds must be adhered to.

These principles would be commonplace and the norm in countries like Canada – but in many countries in the world these standards are often not adhered to.

In addition to these oversights on budgets and finance, parliamentarians should use whatever power and influence they have to safeguard free speech, freedom of the press, and an active civil society of non-governmental organizations. In Canada, members of parliament on the government side shudder when the auditor general publishes his or her quarterly report because the media, the opposition parties and the NGO's have a 'field day' with it, embarrassing the government.

None of this is easy, especially in countries where the executive branch has most of the powers, either constitutionally or by convention through benign neglect. In Canada we are having a similar debate on this topic. The question is – has the Prime Minister's office become too 'presidential'? Many accept that Canada's parliament has allowed the erosion of its power by omission.

In a March 5th 2003 speech I gave to students at Osgoode Hall Law School, I commented on this development as follows:

"I should say at the outset that I am not a great student of parliamentary procedure. My remarks should be seen as those of a general practitioner – someone who was first elected in 1996 – and a witness to the growing concentration of power in the Office of the Prime Minister; together with the concurrent diminishment in the contribution that backbench members of parliament are able to make to the policy-making process.

I am a believer in the need for the executive to govern. In our parliamentary system, which is modeled on the Westminster model or British parliamentary system, the members of the executive, or Cabinet, are, with some exceptions, elected members of parliament. This raises the tension for MP's on the government side to hold the executive accountable to the parliament and people of Canada, while at the same time being supportive of, and expressing confidence in, the government (your colleagues).

The House of Commons has more recently begun to exercise some of the powers that have always been there, but not always employed. A case-in-point is the rejection by the House of Commons of the request by the government for additional funding for the troubled gun registry. Another was the passage by the House of Commons of the motion to have chairs of standing committees of the House elected by secret ballot – thereby allowing members on the government side to vote according to their own wishes rather than adopting the candidate put forward by the government Whip after consulting with the Prime Minister. But more on committee chairs later. The point is that to some extent Canada's parliament has not been exercising the powers that it already possesses. This is true but it is not, in my view, the whole story.

Our former Finance Minister, and Prime Minister, Rt. Hon. Paul Martin, attacked the democratic deficit that had developed – and he was as right on this point as he was when he began his assault on the huge fiscal deficit that we inherited when we came into office in 1993.

I recall the years when I was an assistant deputy minister in the British Columbia Ministry of Forests (from 1980 until 1987). Bill Bennett was premier for much of that time and he had a very distinct approach to governance. His premier's office consisted of a small handful of staff. He delegated day-to-day responsibilities to his ministers. Issues were not 'micro-managed' at the center. If a minister under-performed, he or she was dropped from cabinet. This approach quickly changed in B.C. when Bill Vander Zalm became premier, and was perpetuated with subsequent NDP governments. The premiers' office in B.C. expanded its staff and its role in the overall machinery of government. The same can be said of Mike Harris' premier's office in Ontario. And, the same can be said about the Prime Minister's office in Ottawa – and not just the current Prime Minister. This trend started in Mr. Trudeau's time and was continued by Brian Mulroney and others to the point we are today.

We need to give back some 'power to the people', through their elected representatives. We need to do this without upsetting the careful balance that is needed between the need for the executive branch to govern, and the need for elected representatives to be duly engaged in the democratic decision-making process."

Parliament in Canada, and in most parliamentary democracies, has four separate and distinct responsibilities regarding its accountability over government:
1) It approves legislative requests from government for programs and policies;
2) The government has to seek authority from parliament (ways and means) for its policies on taxation in order to raise the funds necessary for government;
3) The government must seek approval from parliament for spending authority (the Estimates process); and,
4) Government is required to report to parliament and table a variety of reports on its performance.

This oversight role that parliament performs is absolutely crucial, and, if properly exercised, holds the government to account and should result in greater probity and prudence in its spending decisions. Corruption grows wherever accountability is weak.

Parliamentarians can also push for tax and regulatory reform. Those countries with more predictable regulatory regimes and lower levels of regulatory discretion have a better chance of minimizing or eliminating corruption.

Getting the institutions of government right is another area where parliamentarians can make a contribution. Corruption cannot be reined in by repression alone. Countries with presidential or semi-presidential systems have fewer built-in accountability mechanisms than parliamentary systems.

Parliamentarians, knowing that accountability promotes transparency and good governance, are now coming together to form an organization to combat, and speak out, against corrupt activities. The Global Organization of Parliamentarians Against Corruption (GOPAC) was founded in 2002 at a conference hosted by the Canadian House of Commons and Senate.

GOPAC has over 700 members around the world, organised into regional and national chapters. This organization is the umbrella organization to motivate, support, and organize regional chapters around the world such as North American Parliamentarians Against Corruption (NAPAC), Latin American Parliamentarians Against Corruption (LAPAC) Southeast Asian Parliamentarians Against Corruption (SEAPAC), African Parliamentarians Network Against Corruption (APNAC), Arab Parliamentarians Against Corruption (ARPAC), Caribbean Parliamentarians Against Corruption (CaribPAC), European Parliamentarians Against Corruption (EPAC), North East Asian Parliamentarians Against Corruption (NEAPAC), and Newly Independent States Parliamentarians Against Corruption (NISPAC). Other Chapters are being formed on a regular basis. A chapter has been formed in the Russian Federation named Parliamentarians for Parliamentary Control. In fact, a few years ago, a colleague of mine from the House of Commons in Canada (John Williams), and I met with members of the State Duma in Russia on the topic of governance; and this dialogue is continuing amongst parliamentarians and with Canada's Auditor General and Russia's Accounts Chamber. The Canadian International Development Agency (CIDA) through the Parliamentary Centre in Canada is supporting this work.

The mandate of the regional chapter of GOPAC in North America – North American Parliamentarians Against Corruption, or NAPAC, is to:

- Build the capacity of parliaments to exercise accountability with a particular emphasis on financial matters;
- Share information with international parliamentarians about lessons learned and best practices;
- Undertake projects and organize workshops focused on reducing corruption and promoting good governance; and
- Cooperate with International Financial Institutions (IFI's) and organizations in civil society to build on current information and research that is applicable to parliamentarians.

So, parliamentarians are increasingly involving themselves in the fight against bribery, corruption and money laundering.

They better understand the destabilizing influence of bribery and corruption, and the economic costs associated with it. We understand also how the financing of terrorism is a threat to international security. Governments must be held more accountable by parliamentarians and legislate whatever is required, respecting the privacy and human rights of citizens, to stamp out terrorist financing and money laundering. Parliamentarians can work together and with multilateral organizations to find the solutions to these very difficult problems.

For the Thirteenth Annual Session of the Organization for Security and Cooperation in Europe (OSCE) Parliamentary Assembly in July 2005 in Washington DC, USA. I presented the following two resolutions.

The first one addressed corruption and read as follows:

OSCE Parliamentary Assembly

Resolution on the Fight against Corruption

Reiterating that corruption represents one of the major impediments to the prosperity and sustainable development of the participating States, that it undermines their stability and security and threatens the OSCE's shared values,

Reiterating that corruption represents one of the major impediments to the ability of parliaments to represent the citizens of participating States,

Reiterating that no country is free from corruption,

Recognizing that the problem of corruption in societies making a transition from authoritarian regimes is bigger and more difficult as the demands for establishing the rule of law dictate numerous tasks that have to be achieved whilst funds and means are still insufficient,

Determined to further intensify efforts in the implementation of existing OSCE commitments on combating corruption, as reflected in the Charter for European Security adopted at the 1999 OSCE Istanbul Summit and the OSCE Strategy Document for the Economic and Environmental Dimension adopted in Maastricht in 2003,

Reaffirming its commitment to make the elimination of all forms of corruption a priority,

Recalling that the fight against corruption requires the adoption by the parliaments of participating States of a comprehensive and long-term anti-corruption strategy, including anti-corruption laws,

Acknowledging the important work on this issue done by other international organizations, in particular by the United Nations Office on Drugs and Crime (UNODC), the Council of Europe (CoE), the Organisation for Economic Co-operation and Development (OECD), and the Global Organization of Parliamentarians against Corruption,

Recognizing that the United Nations Convention against Corruption, adopted by the General Assembly of the United Nations on 31 October 2003 in New York, marks a major step forward in international co-operation against corruption and provides the opportunity for a global response to the problem,

Reaffirming that the main role of Parliaments in the fight against corruption is the adoption of anti-corruption laws and the empowering of anti-corruption enforcement,

Noting with satisfaction the steps taken by participating legislatures to adopt a comprehensive strategy to combat corruption,

Supporting the efforts of OSCE's offices in assisting participating States' authorities in implementing anti-corruption strategies, notably in Belgrade (Serbia), Yerevan (Armenia), Bishkek (Kyrgyzstan), following the experience gained through the OSCE's Anti-Corruption Campaign in Bosnia and Herzegovina in 2000.

The OSCE Parliamentary Assembly:

Urges parliamentarians of the OSCE participating States to strengthen their efforts to combat corruption and the conditions that foster it,

Urges the parliaments of OSCE participating States, which have not yet done so, to ratify the United Nations Convention against Corruption as soon as possible, in order to ensure its rapid entry into force, and implement it fully,

Calls upon parliamentarians of participating States to promote a positive framework for good governance and public integrity,

> Urges parliaments of participating States to make better use of existing international instruments and assist each other in their fight against corruption,
> Recommends that parliaments of participating States promote the best practices against corruption identified by the OSCE's Office of the Co-ordinator for Economic and Environmental Activities,
> Urges parliaments of participating States to adopt clear and balanced legislative procedures for waiving parliamentary immunities, and to support the establishment of efficient mechanisms for monitoring declarations of income and assets by parliamentarians, ministers, and public servants,
> Recommends that the General Committee on Economic Affairs, Science, Technology, and Environment collaborate with other parliamentary associations and the Global Organization of Parliamentarians against Corruption in developing a programme for parliamentary action against corruption and a document describing the role of parliamentarians in the fight against corruption.

The 2nd resolution focused on the fight against money laundering and read as follows:

> ## OSCE Parliamentary Assembly
> ### Resolution against Money Laundering
> Recognizing that the fight against money laundering is an essential part of the overall struggle to combat the financing of terrorist activity, illegal narcotics trafficking, the activities of organized crime, corruption, and tax evasion,
> Supporting the United Nations Office on Drugs and Crime (UNODC) Global Programme against Money Laundering, and the joint OSCE-UNODC Workshops on Combating Money Laundering and Financing of Terrorism held in Bishkek (Kyrgyzstan), Astana (Kazakhstan), Dushanbe (Tajikistan), Yerevan (Armenia), Baku (Azerbaijan), and Tbilisi (Georgia),
> Noting that money launderers exploit differences among national anti-money laundering systems and move their funds to jurisdictions with ineffective laws,

Supporting the anti-money laundering framework developed by the Financial Action Task Force (FATF) on Money Laundering's *40 Recommendations*,

Noting with satisfaction the existence of legislative tools such as the United Nations Office on Drugs and Crime *Model Money-Laundering, Proceeds of Crime and Terrorist Financing Bill 2003*, 1999 UN *Civil Law Model Law on Laundering, Confiscation and International Cooperation in relation to the Proceeds of Crime*, and the Commonwealth *Model Law for the Prohibition of Money Laundering* of 1996,

Recognizing that the need is greatest in ensuring the appropriate enforcement of anti-corruption laws by competent structures closely monitored by independent bodies that report to the representative parliaments,

The OSCE Parliamentary Assembly:

Urges parliaments of participating States, which have not yet done so, to adopt anti-money laundering laws along the framework developed in the FATF 40 Recommendations, and consistent with the United Nations Office on Drugs and Crime Model *Money-Laundering, Proceeds of Crime and Terrorist Financing Bill 2003*,

Calls upon parliaments of participating States to ensure that adopted legislations are expeditiously enforced, and that the enforcement is adequately monitored by parliamentary bodies,

Encourages parliamentarians to participate in the efforts made by parliamentary associations and international organizations such as the Global Organization of Parliamentarians against Corruption in the fight against money laundering,

Recommends that the General Committee on Economic Affairs, Science, Technology, and Environment collaborate with FATF in identifying parliaments of participating States that have not adopted adequate anti-money laundering laws, or do not have the appropriate tools to monitor the efficient implementation of anti-money laundering laws, and report annually to the Parliamentary Assembly.

I was encouraged by the fact that both these resolutions were passed by the Parliamentary Assembly of the Organization for Security and Cooperation in Europe in Washington D.C. at their session in the summer of 2005. We are continuing to follow-up to ensure that these resolutions don't 'die on the vine' but become living, breathing documents.

On the question of enforcement, the Republic of South Africa has developed an interesting model in the 'Scorpions'. This group, which came into existence in 2001, is a multi-disciplinary agency that investigates and prosecutes organized crime and corruption. With a staff of some 2,000, it is a unit of the National Prosecuting Authority of South Africa. By February 2004, the Scorpions had completed 653 cases, including 380 prosecutions, of which 349 resulted in convictions. This equates to a highly successful conviction rate of 93.1%! When I visited South Africa in September 2006, the anecdotal evidence gleaned from conversations with average citizens was that the Scorpions were serving a useful purpose and were achieving results (notwithstanding the fact that Deputy President Jacob Zuma was acquitted of the corruption charges against him).

In Mexico City, on March 2/3, 2006 the Global Organization of Parliamentarians Against Corruption (GOPAC), and the Senate of Mexico, hosted an Anti Money Laundering Training (AML) workshop for Latin American and Caribbean Parliamentarians. This seminar brought together parliamentarians from across the Latin American and Caribbean region in the Senate of Mexico (Mexico City) for a two day capacity building seminar on anti-money laundering initiatives and combating the financing of terrorism. The seminar was funded by the Canadian Department of Foreign Affairs, Human Security Program, and Scotiabank and was hosted by the Senate of Mexico. Under the leadership of Senator César Jauregui (host) and me, and with contributions from a number of technical experts, parliamentarians undertook discussions on anti-corruption, AML and FT (Financing of Terrorism) and the role/importance of parliamentarians, as well as a comprehensive approach to the UN international treaties and conventions and Financial Action Task Force (FATF) recommendations. The emphasis of the program on the one hand was on improving the understanding on the part of parliamentarians of money laundering, its impacts, and international and national initiatives in the region to combat it. On the other hand, it was to develop an understanding of what parliamentarians could do to help combat money laundering.

The result we were seeking from the seminar was to have participants develop and propose an action plan for the Latin American and Caribbean regions for consideration by the Latin American Parliamentarians Against Corruption (LAPAC) and the Caribbean Parliamentarians Against Corruption (CaribPAC) chapters, and if accepted, implemented by those chapters.

Participants concluded that the best way to achieve this result would be to develop a single resolution proposing a series of actions at both the global and regional levels. The resolution produced by the end of the seminar was signed by nearly all of the parliamentary participants present.

The resolution adopted was as follows –

Resolution of the participants from the GOPAC Anti-Money Laundering Seminar for Latin American and Caribbean Parliamentarians

Recognising that the fight against money laundering is common to all countries of the world and that the fight against money laundering needs to be global in nature.

Recognising that money laundering is a problem that affects the democratic system and social and economic development of all our countries.

Recognising the need to create common standards, adopt best practices and encourage cooperation amongst states and financial institutions.

Recognising that the fight against money laundering needs to be assumed preferably by parliamentarians and parliaments of the Latin American and Caribbean region.

Recognising that the Inter American Convention Against Corruption does not specifically address money laundering.

Resolve to:

i) Strongly encourage the Global Organisation of Parliamentarians Against Corruption (GOPAC) -Anti Money Laundering Initiative, to work with experts in the field to create an international treaty which when adopted would ensure harmonization of AML legislation throughout the world.
ii) Such a treaty would incorporate standardized best practices from around the world.
iii) Work with organizations such as GOPAC, LAPAC, CaribPAC and their associated organizations to build political will to fight corruption and money laundering and implement common international strategies.
iv) Work with organizations such as International Compliance Association, Financial Action Task Force and their associated organizations on increasing the technical capacity to fight corruption and money laundering.
v) Work with parliamentarians from across the globe to raise awareness amongst citizens and the media of the harmful effects of the crime of money laundering and corruption and the role of parliamentarians in reducing the problem.
vi) Legislate to achieve the recovery of the proceeds of these illegal activities.
vii) Recommend a review of the Inter American Convention Against Corruption to include a more explicit acknowledgment of the need to implement anti money laundering regimes.
viii) Investigate including corruption and the laundering of money as international crimes.

What do these resolutions mean and what purpose do they serve? Before I attempt to answer this, one more set of resolutions! The resolutions which follow were adopted at the 2nd Global Conference of the Global Organization of Parliamentarians Against Corruption (GOPAC) that was held in Arusha, Tanzania September 20th-23rd, 2006. This very successful conference had approximately 300 individuals in attendance – mostly Parliamentarians from around the world and members of GOPAC. The Conference was organized into eight working groups. I had the honour to chair the anti-money laundering workshop so the resolution that was adopted by this working group (task force) is presented here also.

2nd Global Conference, Arusha Tanzania
CONFERENCE DECLARATION

The Global Organization of Parliamentarians Against Corruption held its 2nd global conference in Arusha, Tanzania from September 20-23rd. At that conference the delegates, after vigorous debate and discussion, set out a clear vision for the organization.
GOPAC is an organisation committed to leadership for results and has resolved to set up global task forces to energize the debate on issues such as

> Parliamentary Oversight
> Parliamentary Immunity
> Codes of Conduct for Parliamentarians
> Access to Information and Media
> International Conventions Against Corruption
> Anti Money Laundering **
> Resource Revenue Transparency
> Development Assistance Loans and Grants

GOPAC is speaking to the world, saying that these serious political issues need to be addressed. We are prepared to address them.

We call on all governments and other organizations who are committed to good governance, improved prosperity and better lives for their citizens and society to join forces with GOPAC to achieve these objectives.

** details of the anti-money laundering resolution follows on the next page.

AML (Anti Money Laundering), CFT (Combating the Financing of Terrorism), RAA (Recovery of Associated Assets) (Resolution adopted in Arusha Tanzania).

Recognizing:

- the importance of reducing the opportunities for corruption as a result of the laundering of money by eliminating the capacity to illegally obtain funds for personal use or terrorism; and
- the need for international cooperation to address money laundering and the repatriation of associated assets.

GOPAC resolves to:

- extend the GOPAC global Task Force of GOPAC members to guide this work and advise the GOPAC Executive of further steps needed as well as how this can complement Control of Terrorist Financing initiatives.
- encourage training of parliamentarians in all chapters to expose larger numbers of parliamentarians to the issues and steps governments and parliamentarians need to take – based on the pilot training initiatives GOPAC has undertaken in cooperation with WB, IMF and the International Compliance Association.
- develop awareness amongst GOPAC members of the FATF 40 + 9 recommendations.
- seek 'observer' status in the FATF.
- examine the benefits of drafting and encouraging the adoption of an International Convention Against Money Laundering while encouraging countries to ratify and implement the UN Convention Against Corruption.
- that GOPAC begin dialogue with the offshore and international banking community to: (a) better understand what the community is doing to fight money laundering and the financing of terrorism, and; (b) develop protocols specifically on fighting the laundering and the recovery of corrupt money and assets.

The resolutions that were adopted in Mexico City were important in themselves but what was equally powerful was the media coverage of the event. The efforts of Senator César Jauregui of Mexico paid off and the national and local media provided extensive coverage of our meetings in Mexico City and the resolution that was passed. The benefit of this type of media attention is that it raises the level of consciousness of the public of the level of corruption and money laundering, and also of the remedies that are needed to address these related problems. Public awareness usually results in pressure on elected officials and a call to action. If nothing else, when Parliamentarians convene to discuss corruption and money laundering, a more knowledgeable public results and citizens become more engaged in the issues.

With respect to the specific resolutions adopted in Mexico City, three require some elaboration. The first resolution calls for GOPAC to investigate the adoption of an international treaty on money laundering that would lead to a harmonization of anti-money laundering worldwide. Money launderers move their activities into those jurisdictions where the anti-money laundering legislation and enforcement is weak. The old adage 'a chain is as good as its weakest link' is very appropriate here. An international treaty or convention, with the means to enforce, could go some way to closing these gaps. One needs to be careful here, however, not to weaken the standards that the Financial Action Task Force (FATF) is striving to have adopted worldwide. In negotiating an international convention, there is a danger that standards agreed to will be weakened to fit the lowest common denominator. Clearly, this would be counterproductive and is to be avoided at all costs. In this regard, the FATF needs to broaden and extend its influence so that all countries will employ the needed international anti-money laundering standards.

In Mexico City we resolved to legislate to recover the proceeds of corrupt activities that have been laundered to conceal their identity. This is becoming a bigger issue, and one where expertise is developing quickly. GOPAC is pursuing this with the offshore and international banking community (more on this later).

GOPAC has concluded that designating corruption and money laundering as international crimes, while perhaps laudable in its intent, may be over-reaching and very difficult to achieve. While it is true that the impact on citizens of corruption and money laundering are very negative and far-reaching, it may not be possible or appropriate to put these crimes on a par with genocide and mass murder.

The GOPAC resolutions adopted in Arusha, Tanzania in September 2006 were most encouraging and covered the full landscape of the problems and issues. For each of the eight working groups (now task forces) an action plan is being developed, resources being sought, and results expected when GOPAC hosts its 3rd Global Conference in 2008 in the middle east. I have been asked to lead the task force on money laundering so I have chosen to focus on the resolutions of this working group that were adopted unanimously in Arusha.

With these resolutions, GOPAC has committed itself to creating awareness amongst its members of the 40 + 9 recommendations of the Financial Action Task Force (FATF). GOPAC acknowledges that the FATF is the anti-money laundering standard setter. GOPAC has begun to build more awareness by encouraging its regional chapters to create linkages with the FATF style regional organizations, which are present throughout the world, and begin working with these organizations to develop and implement anti-money laundering strategies.

GOPAC has also asked the FATF for observer status on the Financial Action Task Force. This would allow parliamentarians a more direct role and impact on the development of anti-money laundering standards, and implementation tools.

In the last GOPAC anti-money laundering resolution, GOPAC commits itself to dialoguing with the offshore and international banking community with the objective of limiting or eliminating the laundering of corrupt funds through financial institutions such as these. GOPAC has begun this process by contacting the Offshore Group of Banking Supervisors (see letter which follows).

GLOBAL ORGANIZATION OF PARLIAMENTARIANS AGAINST CORRUPTION
ORGANIZATION MONDIALE DES PARLEMENTAIRES CONTRE LA CORRUPTION
ORGANIZACIÓN MUNDIAL DE PARLAMENTARIOS CONTRA LA CORRUPCIÓN

August 13, 2007

Mr. Colin Powell
Chair
Offshore Group of Banking Supervisors
PO Box 267
Nelson House.
David Place
St Helier
Jersey, JE4 8TP
Channel Islands

Dear Mr. Powell:

Allow me first to introduce myself. My name is Roy Cullen and I serve as Member of Parliament in the House of Commons, in Ottawa, Canada. I am writing to you in my capacity as the leader of the Global Anti Money Laundering Initiative of the Global Organisation of Parliamentarians Against Corruption (GOPAC). GOPAC is an international network of over seven hundred members of parliament in over seventy countries. It is the basic objective of GOPAC to make parliaments work as effective institutions of oversight of their governments, and to fight corruption. Corruption and money laundering are viewed by GOPAC and its members as clearly linked and as unjust, de-stabilizing and economically inappropriate activities that wreak havoc on a country and its inhabitants.

The following is a brief summary of GOPAC and its focus. More information can be obtained from our web site www.gopacnetwork.org. To achieve our objective, we have three agendas that form the bedrock of the organization:

    1) *Peer support of parliamentarians* who are engaged in the fight against corruption. It is necessary for parliamentarians to know that they do not stand alone when travelling the sometimes lonely and

difficult road in their fight against corruption and money laundering. Peer support includes mentoring by informed Members of Parliament with others, especially new parliamentarians, on the role of Parliament as the institution of accountability and oversight of government - on behalf of all the citizens of their jurisdiction.

2) *Education programs for parliamentarians* on a more formal basis to, again, help them understand their role as overseers of government. We send our young people to university to become lawyers, doctors, engineers, accountants etc., but with absolutely no training or specific education, we expect parliamentarians to be highly competent and professional in the oversight of their nation's business. Our Anti Money Laundering Initiative (AMLI) is a key component of this agenda because parliamentarians around the world clearly understand, and have witnessed, the link between corruption and money laundering.

3) *Leadership for Results* by identifying clear objectives starting with small steps and goals on what can be achieved in the fight against corruption and money laundering. By measuring the accomplishments of these steps and goals, GOPAC and its chapters will be able to demonstrate effectiveness as an organization.

Parliamentarians throughout the world have expressed a strong desire to obtain further information and training in money laundering; in particular, what legislative and other tools are available to them so that they can assist in the reduction or elimination of money laundering in their respective countries.

GOPAC and its members have been engaged in the fight against Money Laundering since 2003. The organization has held workshops in East Africa (2003), Latin America and the Caribbean (2005, 2006) and Eastern Europe (2005) that have provided parliamentarians with key information and access to resources, to assist them in the fight against money laundering and the financing of terrorism. We have also discussed – parliamentarians to parliamentarians – how to build an effect AML/CFT regime and at the same time address the political dimension of this sometimes daunting task.

Most recently, we held an AML workshop with parliamentarians from around the world as part of the 2nd GOPAC Global Conference in Arusha, Tanzania. This workshop included panelists representing the World Bank, International

Monetary Fund (IMF), Financial Action Task Force (FATF) and the Egmont Group. The resolution produced was approved of by all of the participants attending the Conference.

As part of this resolution, which is attached for your information, you will note that the GOPAC members have asked us to begin a dialogue with the offshore banking group. Given the OGBS's stated aims *to participate with relevant international organisations in setting and promoting the implementation of international standards for cross-border banking supervision, and for combating money laundering/terrorist financing* and *encourage members to apply high standards of supervision based on internationally accepted principle*, I foresee many areas of potential collaboration. In particular, GOPAC is interested in slowing or eliminating the laundering of corrupt money and in recovering these national assets. While recognizing the complexity and challenges, GOPAC would like to work with your organization to achieve the same degree of enhanced cooperation that your members have accomplished in the fight against terrorist financing and drug crimes and enhance this cooperation to the fight against the laundering of corrupt money.

It would be greatly appreciated if I might receive more information on the activities of the OGBS. I look forward to discussing our mutual initiatives further.

Regards,

Hon. Roy Cullen, MP
Chair, AML, GOPAC

Parliamentarians can also support their governments in their efforts to assist developing countries and emerging economies to build capacity in local institutions, to develop sound governance models that work, and to assist with legislative solutions, as they are required.

For the last five years the Parliamentary Network of the World Bank has been in operation and growing in its influence and effectiveness.

The purpose of the Parliamentary Network on the World Bank (PNoWB) is to increase parliamentary involvement and effectiveness in the field of international development.

The core mission of the PNoWB is fivefold:

1) *Accountability*: To facilitate and encourage direct policy dialogue between Parliamentarians and multilateral development institutions to provide greater transparency of World Bank policies and practices and increase collective accountability.
2) *Advocacy*: To provide the members of the Network with a platform for coordinated parliamentary advocacy on international development issues.
3) *Networking*: To encourage concerted action, early debate and exchange of information among Parliamentarians on major issues of international development, finance and poverty eradication.
4) *Partnerships*: To take initiatives to further co-operation and encourage partnerships between parliamentarians and policy makers, the academic community, the business sector and non-governmental organizations on development issues.
5) *Progress Review*: To promote the development of parliamentary mechanisms and practices for the effective democratic control of development assistance in all its phases.

To achieve these objectives, the PNoWB delivers the following programs:

- *Annual Conference*: At least once a year the Network organizes a conference. This is organized in partnership with the parliament of the host country and the World Bank.
- *Field Trips*: The Network facilitates field trips for parliamentarians

from donor countries to visit projects in developing countries. At the same time the Network organizes visits from parliamentarians from developing countries to parliaments in countries with well-established democratic traditions.
- *Website*: The Network has its own website in order to facilitate coalition building and the exchange of information on international development issues among parliamentarians and multilateral institutions such as the World Bank (www.pnowb.org).
- *Consultations*: The PNoWB engages in consultations with the World Bank and other international financial institutions on their respective projects, programs, and research activities.
- *Training*: The Network seeks training opportunities for parliamentarians, in partnership with the World Bank Institute, amongst others, on the Bank's technical procedures.
- *Newsletter*: A newsletter is disseminated regularly to inform members about the activities of the Network and to raise its profile vis-à-vis third parties. The newsletter features, inter alia, interviews with parliamentarians active in international development.
- *Research*: The Network encourages small-scale, parliament-specific research projects based on the needs defined by the members of the Network.
- *Partnerships*: The Network actively seeks opportunities to build partnerships with other international parliamentary networks to encourage cross-fertilization. In addition, the Network attempts to build bridges with other constituencies involved in international development (academia, NGOs, etc.).

This type of parliamentary interaction with the World Bank, and increasingly with other institutions like the International Monetary Fund, can be useful accountability mechanisms for elected officials. It provides them with an opportunity to dialogue with these institutions and provide them with feedback on priorities and best practices.

There are many ways in which parliamentarians can demand greater accountability from the executive branch of government. After a two-year debate in the Parliament of Canada, I was able to have my private member's bill, an act respecting user fees, enacted by parliament and brought into force in March 2004. The intent of this legislation is to bring greater transparency and accountability and parliamentary oversight to federal government departments and agencies when they attempt to recover costs through user fees.

User fees take many different forms and are meant to defray some or all of the costs of a service provided by government presumably in the public interest, but which also provides a specific service to the client (for example license fees, registrations, etc.). In 2003/4 these user fees amounted to approximately $6 billion across the entire federal government. These fees, while not taxes per se, are akin to taxes and they are priced by monopolies. If you want a new drug approved in Canada one can't shop around for the best deal – you are obliged to work with Health Canada. Likewise, if you want a Canadian passport you must deal with the Department of Foreign Affairs.

I have always pointed out that I support the federal government's objective to recover costs through user fees for private goods or proprietary services. The focus of my private member's bill was on the following concerns:

- The need for more parliamentary oversight when user fees are introduced or changed;
- The need for greater stakeholder participation in the fee-setting process;
- Improved linkages between user fees, and federal department and agency performance specifications and standards;
- The requirement for more comprehensive stakeholder impact and competitiveness analysis when new user fees, or fee increases, are contemplated;
- The goal of increased transparency with respect to why fees are applicable, what fees are charged, what costs are identified as recoverable, and whether performance standards are being met;
- The need for an independent dispute resolution process to address the complaints or grievances of the payers of user fees; and
- The need for an annual report outlining all user fees in effect that

would be tabled in the House of Commons, and referred to the appropriate Committee of the House (Finance).

I believe my bill will accomplish these objectives, but at the time of writing, federal government departments and agencies were in the process of digesting how they would implement the spirit, intent and letter of this new law of Canada. This legislation somewhat limits the ability of the executive branch of government, and at the same time it empowers parliamentarians. Small steps are sometimes needed to accomplish the overall mission!

This was what an editorial writer for the National Post had to say about my Bill (before it was passed into law):

User fees are just another tax grab
By Neville Nankivell Staff Writer

So-called private member's bills introduced by backbenchers usually don't get far in Parliament. Some aren't even designated as votable. But Bill C-212 on government user fees is -- and deserves all-party support. It would make user charges for government-provided services subject to parliamentary scrutiny and approval, the same as required for taxes.

There's growing and legitimate discontent in the business community over the explosion in government user fees imposed on companies in recent years. Many businesses regard steep increases in what's charged as an unfair tax grab.

Introduced last fall by Toronto-area Liberal MP Roy Cullen, the proposed legislation would make Parliament rather than government departments and agencies ultimately responsible for approving new user fees or raising existing ones. It would ensure public debate over whether services delivered actually give value for money.

There has been a big increase in user fees for a diverse range of government services since the mid-1990s when an aggressive departmental cost-recovery program was launched as part of Ottawa's deficit reduction plan. The intention was sensible -- to defray the costs of government services that provided a commercial and sometimes exclusive benefit to businesses. Examples: food safety inspections, ice-breaking operations, pharmaceutical product approvals, some kinds of weather forecasting.

Fees were only supposed to be charged if there was a direct business or individual benefit from the government-provided service. The trouble was that government departments used the umbrella of deficit reduction to go on a user-fee spree. Ottawa now rakes in $4-billion a year in fees levied by about 50 departments and agencies in connection with some 400 cost-recovery programs. Many charges were set by way of regulation with little real consultation on their business impact or how they compared internationally.

This raised the hackles of many business groups. They don't think departmental officials have properly justified the level of new or increased user charges or done enough analysis of how they affect business competitiveness. They also accuse some departments of just trying to expand revenues without caring about an adequate relationship between what's charged and the cost and quality of the delivered service. It's also not as if businesses have a lot of choice in the matter. Government departments are often the sole providers of necessary services. Certain kinds of companies couldn't stay in business without them. An example: mandatory food safety inspection services.

Business groups also complain that, in some cases, while fees have gone up, services have deteriorated. As an example, they say charges introduced in 1996 for reviewing new veterinary drug submissions are twice as high here as in Britain or Australia, but the process now takes twice as long as it did in the mid-1990s.

More than two years ago the all-party parliamentary Finance committee also was highly critical of the fee-setting process and made several recommendations for change. These included giving departments less autonomy to impose user fees and setting up an independent dispute resolution process. However, the federal Treasury Board, which has an important role in the government's financial affairs, pretty much rejected all the committee's main proposals. This dismissal came despite criticisms of the present system by the Auditor General of Canada.

Meanwhile, business groups continue to object, through a Business Coalition on Cost Recovery group that represents 15 industry associations. Garth Whyte, executive vice-president of the Canadian Federation of Independent Business, says that, like most other associations, his small-business organization supports user-pay cost recovery in principle. But hefty increases in the fees are hurting many small firms, he says, and in some cases companies are required to take services they do not want or need. Business groups are also concerned about cross-subsidization of government services. And they want more adequate notification of intentions to set, raise or broaden user charges.

Mr. Cullen's bill addresses these issues. It has support in principle from the opposition parties and from many other Liberal MPs. They agree that some user fees are much higher than the cost of services provided and that many services are not cost effective. Some have labelled user fees as hidden taxes or a tax with another name.

The government itself admits faults with the present system. It acknowledges that improvements can be made to the system and it wants more explicit guidelines for departments and agencies. A revised policy is being worked on and should be announced soon. But the government's executive branch remains loath to give parliamentary committees the right to approve the setting and amending of fees for government-provided services. It prefers ministers to retain this responsibility.

The crux of the problem is that present policy is vague, fee setting is inconsistent and the government has been reviewing the issue for long enough. At the very least, it should agree to some form of mandatory ongoing parliamentary oversight on user fees and an independent dispute settlement system. Better still would be all-party co-operation in making Mr. Cullen's constructive bill workable, then get it passed and give Parliament a wider role in how government raises revenues.

It is sometimes argued that corruption is a cultural matter or endemic in certain societies. Maybe so, but that doesn't make it right! It just tells that it will be more difficult and take more time to route out. The INDEM Foundation in a 2001 report entitled Russia Anti-corruption Diagnostics: Sociological Analysis argues, "Corruption is little more than a social phenomenon, admittedly a very significant and harmful one."

Elected officials have a large responsibility to take steps to ensure that bribery and corruption is not accepted as a societal norm. This can be accomplished in a number of ways. First and foremost we must lead by example; i.e. as elected people we should reject bribery and corruption and refuse to be a party to it. Elected officials can take a number of other steps – for example by ensuring that public servants are paid an adequate wage and have reasonable job security – so they can have the confidence to reject bribes. In some countries, such salaries and wages are kept deliberately low because public servants are expected to take bribes. This approach has to stop. Citizens are paying for this either way – either as an 'on-site' user fee or as a general tax.

Emigration and Globalization: More people are on the Move

Why do people leave the country of their birth in search of the Promised Land? If such a paradise were at home, would they emigrate? Some understandably leave because they are legitimate refugees, fleeing from repressive regimes, civil war and the like. Some wish to be re-united with family members who have already left their home country and settled in a new land. The predominant reason, however, for uprooting from one's home country, where one is familiar and comfortable with the language, religion and culture is usually economic in nature. People leave because the economic prospects in their own country are seen to be inferior to the prospects abroad in another country. Corruption in their home country and income inequalities are contributing factors to be sure.

In a recent Working Paper prepared for the United Nations High Commissioner for Refugees (UNHCR), the following trends were described:

"The number of long-term international migrants (that is, those residing in foreign countries for more than one year) has grown steadily in the past four decades. According to the UN Population Division, in 1965, only 15 million persons fit the definition, rising to 84 million by 1975 and 105 million by 1985. There were an estimated 120 million international migrants in 1990, the last year for which detailed international statistics are available. An examination of data from selected countries of in-migration indicates that international migration continued with about the same rate of growth in the 1990s. As of the year 2000, according to estimates prepared by this author for the International Organisation for Migration, there are 150 million international migrants."[104]

The report continues: "Between 1965 and 1915, the growth in international migration (1.16% per year) did not keep pace with the growth in global population (2.04% per year). However, overall population growth began to decline in the 1980s while international migration continued to increase significantly. During the period from 1985 to 1990, global population growth increased by about 1.1 percent per year, whereas the total population of international migrants increased by 2.59 percent per

---

[104] Susan F. Martin, *New Issues in Refugee Research,* Working Paper No. 41 prepared for UNHCR, Global Migration Trends and Asylum, April 2001, p. 2.

year. Even with the numbers of international migrants large and growing, it is important to keep in mind that fewer than three percent of the world's population have been living outside of their home country for a year or longer. The propensity to move internationally, particularly in the absence of compelling reasons such as wars, is limited to a small proportion of humans. International migrants come from all parts of the world and they go to all parts of the world. In fact, few countries are unaffected by international migration. Many countries are sources of international flows, while others are net receivers and still others are transit countries through which migrants reach receiving countries. Such countries as Mexico experience migration in all three capacities, as source, receiving and transit countries.

Migration tends to be within regions, with migrants often remaining within the same continent. More than half of international migrants traditionally have moved from one developing country to another. In recent years, however, migration from poorer to richer countries has increased significantly. While the traditional immigration countries (the United States, Canada and Australia) continue to see large-scale movements, as a result of labour recruitment that began in the 1960s and 1970s, Europe, the oil rich Persian Gulf states and the 'economic tigers' of east and Southeast Asia are now also major destinations for international migrants.

The industrialised countries belonging to the Organisation for Economic Cooperation and Development (OECD) experienced significant growth in their immigrant population during the 1990s. In 1986/87, about 36 million international migrants (some of whom subsequently naturalized) lived in the US, France, Germany, Canada, Australia and the United Kingdom. A decade later, more than 46 million international migrants were reported to be living in these same countries, more than a 25 percent increase.

The most rapid growth in the number of international migrants tends to occur as a result of refugee crises. Massive numbers of refugees may cross a border within a very short time, often into areas with little prior immigration. The more than 800,000 refugees who fled from Kosovo to Albania and the former Yugoslav Republic of Macedonia in 1999 represent one of the most recent manifestations of this phenomenon."[105]

The report continues: "In addition to legal avenues of entry for labour migrants is unauthorised migration. Statistics on unauthorised migration are hard to find in most countries since these movements are generally clandestine, but it appears that the numbers are substantial. Unauthorised workers can be found in almost as diverse a range of jobs and industries as authorized workers, with agricultural and food processing jobs, light manufacturing, construction and service jobs being the most common types of employment. In many cases, unauthorised migrants are smuggled into countries by professional rings that specialize in human trafficking."[106]

This migration comes at a great social and economic cost as the following commentary in a UNHCR report indicates: "There is no question that the number of those seeking asylum in developed countries increased substantially over the past two decades. In 2000, just over 400,000 persons applied for asylum in the 15 countries of the European Union (EU), double the number in 1980, but down from a high of 700,000 in 1992. With the increase in asylum seekers comes an increase in expenditures to pay for refugee status determination procedures and for the social assistance provided to asylum seekers. By one estimate, that expense among developed countries around the world reached $10 billion in 2000. When only one-quarter of asylum seekers is ultimately granted refugee status, as happened in the EU in 1999, governments balk."[107]

In my riding of Etobicoke North in Toronto, according to the 2001 census, 56.5% of the population were recent immigrants to Canada. The largest of these groups was from South Asia (India, Pakistan, Sri Lanka, etc.). While it is true that some of these people emigrated to Canada because of conflicts in their home country (this is particularly true for the many Tamils in my riding from Sri Lanka) the majority came to Canada in search of a better life and improved standard of living. We are blessed with their decision to make their new home in Canada because they add character and diversity to our Canadian mosaic, but one can't help but wonder that if corruption and poverty in their home countries

---

[105] Susan F. Martin, *New Issues in Refugee Research*, Working Paper No. 41 prepared for UNHCR, Global Migration Trends and Asylum, April 2001, p. 3.

[106] Ibid, p. 5.

[107] UNHCR web site.

were factors in their decisions, and if they would have preferred to stay in their countries of birth had it not been for the lack of opportunity and injustice they experienced. I have heard countless anecdotal stories from individuals such as this who were tired and utterly discouraged by the levels of poverty and corruption in countries like India and Pakistan and how this prompted them to seek a better life in Canada.

Their loss is our gain but in the 'big picture' this type of migration must cause to reflect on the social and economic costs associated with trends like this.

CHAPTER 6

HOW DO WE MOVE FORWARD? – THE 20 POINT PLAN

We need to attack the challenges of poverty and corruption in different ways. The old methods have yielded some limited success in reducing poverty, but the results have been very modest. Conventional wisdoms need to be re-visited and new paradigms developed. While the traditional approaches to overseas development assistance have evolved over the years, they do not appear to have had the intended impact. Direct international aid evolved to a philosophy focused on 'giving a fishing rod – not the fish – so that people in poor countries can learn to fish for themselves.'

In the late 1980's, management consulting projects took me to the Northwest Territories of Canada. Here I learned at a practical level what I had known intuitively; that is, the importance for people who are in receipt of aid, of any description, to take an interest and make their own commitment to any supported projects and initiatives. At the time of my visits to Yellowknife in the Northwest Territories, the Northwest Territories Housing Corporation had two distinct housing programs for aboriginal Canadians. One program could be characterized as a typical social housing program – fully subsidized housing for poor aboriginal families. The second program was what was referred to as the 'sweat equity' program. In this program, the Northwest Territories Housing Corporation provided the building materials to an aboriginal individual who was willing to build the house for himself or herself – hence the term 'sweat equity'. I was told that the houses occupied in the first category were in a state of disrepair, whereas the 'sweat equity' houses were well maintained and cared for. This is not surprising when you think about it. Given human nature, people are more inclined to care for things when a part of them is injected into the project. I believe there are lessons to be learned here in our approach to international development aid. It is better when the local aid recipients are partners in the enterprise or project.

Another good example of local empowerment and civic society is in the Brazilian town of Porte Allegri. In brief, a new constitution was drafted for the city, which gave more power to local government, and for citizen councils to have more input into the policies and programs of their federal government. Through a series of assemblies, delegates were chosen to represent the 16 districts in the Porte Allegri area. The citizens themselves were able also to decide how the budget would be spent. Since 1988 the city has made a significant dent in poverty with 98% of the residences currently having running water, paved roads, higher enrolment of education, and a reduction in corruption.[108] These results underline the importance of community-tailored solutions, rather than the traditional macro-oriented top-down approaches which often neglect how and why poor people are doing what they are doing.

There have also been attempts to tie aid to the procurement of related goods and services from the donor country. This is still a contentious area for debate. My own view is that tied aid is acceptable provided pricing and quality are competitive. In Canada our 'tied aid' program has been delivered by CIDA Inc. – an arm of the Canadian International Development Agency. Development experts at Canada's embassies and missions abroad speak consistently of the positive aspects of CIDA Inc. projects. These projects have often involved small and medium-sized enterprises in Canada and, given our large multi-cultural community, this program seems to be a 'natural' for our country. We are able to draw on the knowledge and experience of our local population with the customs and traditions of the countries of their birth and translate this into highly productive and mutually beneficial development projects.

Aid promised on the condition that the developing country commits to a set of public policies acceptable to the donor country or multilateral

---

[108] Juan Marsiaj, *Local Empowerment in Civic Society,* Lecture for POL210Y1 Politics of Development: Issues and Challenges, Isabelle Bader Theatre, University of Toronto, Toronto, 23 March 2004.

agencies such as the World Bank, is often the way in which development projects or financial assistance packages from the IMF proceed. This policy of 'conditionality' is also a highly contentious one, and one that has created much negative publicity for organizations like the IMF and World Bank. In a June, 2002 address I made at the Parliamentary Assembly of the Council of Europe, I commented on the role of the World Bank and IMF as follows:

"Globalization is a frequently used word, which means very different things to different people. To some, globalization is the natural and obvious extension of a shrinking world, faster communications and the tearing down of tariff protection walls. Most, if not all, economists would argue that the elimination of tariffs has the effect of significantly increasing incomes and wealth. To others, globalization is the monopolization of income and wealth creation by multinationals and political elites – to the detriment of the many.

The more recent debate on globalization contains some ironies. The Breton Woods institutions, namely the International Monetary Fund and the World Bank, were created to help all countries share in the benefits of global trade and commerce. This may be hard to believe as we have witnessed the protests during the last few years by so-called civil society at meetings of these institutions. I say so-called civil society because some of these groups, albeit a minority, support violence to achieve their objectives – not exactly a civilised response however noble the objective.

Where have we gone wrong as elected representatives to allow that level of distrust and lack of confidence, by some, in our international financial institutions? Is it a lack of transparency by these institutions that has led to misunderstandings or have the actions, or lack of action, by the international financial institutions been the cause of this level of animosity?

The role and reform of the international financial institutions have been a long-standing Canadian concern. Indeed Canada made international financial issues a central focus of a previous G7/G8 summit, which it hosted in Halifax in 1995, and Canadian parliamentarians also made a number of reform proposals in preparing for that summit. As you know, Canada is again hosting the G8 summit this year. G7 finance ministers met again in Halifax just a few weeks ago. And tomorrow is the first day of the summit, convening in Kananaskis, Alberta, where G8 leaders are addressing several key themes that relate to the mandates of the IMF and the World Bank – namely, sustaining global economic growth, and realising a new development partnership with the continent of Africa.

Once again, Canadian parliamentarians have been involved in preparing ideas for the summit. At the request of our Prime Minister, the House of Commons' Standing Committee on Foreign Affairs and International Trade – the former chair of which is now Canada's Minister of Foreign Affairs – undertook public consultations across the country and tabled a report on summit priorities in early June. There are similarities with some of the recommendations addressed by the rapporteur, Mr Gusenbauer, in the areas of international finance, development assistance, debt and trade.

Canada's former finance minister, Paul Martin, has provided leadership and energy to the Heavily Indebted Poor Countries Initiative, but more needs to be done. We need to understand better what factors determine the sustainability of debt levels. We must provide assistance to poor countries in identifying debt capacities, and with debt management strategies. Transparent and accountable governance, and anti-corruption measures, need to be at the forefront of debt forgiveness.

With regard to the provision of concessional finance for low-income countries, notably in Africa, Canada was able to broker a compromise at the G7 finance ministers meeting in Halifax several weeks ago, when they endorsed a full replenishment of the International Development Association, with a limited increase in the use of grants to the 18 to 21% range, to enhance, as their statement put it, 'the effectiveness of IDA in helping the poorest and debt vulnerable countries combat HIV/AIDS, support the social sectors including education, and overcome the effects of devastating conflict.'

With respect to promoting greater transparency and stability within the international financial system as a whole, Canada's former finance minister Paul Martin has been at the forefront of proposals at the IMF and World Bank, and through leadership in the G7, G20, and the

Financial Stability Forum among others. The objective is to put in place mechanisms for better early warning systems, more timely and orderly resolution of sovereign-debt financial crises and greater private sector participation in that process.

The rapporteur's analysis would seem to support the compelling case which former Canadian finance minister Paul Martin has made for measures including debt repayment standstills, and collective action clauses in loan contracts that would make it easier to renegotiate debts which become unpayable, but also putting up-front limits on the amount of any future financial bailouts. The rapporteur supports the concept of an international bankruptcy court, which could lay down clear rules and expectations to apply to cases of sovereign debt crises – similar to existing domestic regimes governing financial failures. At the same time, some Canadian non-governmental organisations which support such a debt arbitration mechanism have also argued for it to be independent of IMF control since the Fund is itself a creditor and may be subject to the political direction of its largest shareholder, the United States.

Combating money laundering and the financing of terrorism remain important challenges. Canada has recently enacted anti-money laundering legislation, and the agency responsible for its implementation, FINTRAC, is now in operation.

Finally, I would like to note the work of the Toronto International Leadership Centre for Financial Supervision, which was established in 1997 by the World Bank and the Canadian Government. Strengthening financial sector regulation and supervision is obviously an important objective that is especially needed in crisis economies. So far the Toronto Centre has provided training to nearly 400 senior public officials in more than 100 countries, and has recently also begun joint programmes with the Financial Stability Institute in Basle, Switzerland.

The work of achieving a sound, equitable, socially and environmentally sustainable international economy is far from over. The IMF and the World Bank must continue to adapt and to reform themselves so that they are more transparent and accountable, and therefore better able to respond to the critical developments and new challenges which have been so astutely identified by the rapporteur. 'Cookie cutter' solutions will no longer work. IFI's will need to play the innovative and global public interest role that is expected of them.

As parliamentarians we can, and should, play a key role in this evolution."

Here are some of the areas I believe we need to focus on if we are to significantly reduce poverty and corruption in the years ahead:

1. Make corruption a crime against humanity.

When one evaluates the havoc that corruption wreaks on a nation, it is easy to understand why a parliamentarian from an African country at a meeting in Ottawa suggested that corruption should be designated by the United Nations as a crime against humanity. While it is always difficult and dangerous to equate economic crimes with crimes like genocide, murder and rape, the negative impact that corruption has on a country's citizens cannot be underestimated.

2. Implement an international treaty to combat money laundering.

While there have been a number of international conventions and treaties on bribery and corruption (e.g. UN Convention Against Corruption (UNCAC), OECD Convention on Bribery and Corruption) the international efforts against the related problem of money laundering have been more regional (e.g. work of the Council of Europe on the fight against money laundering).

One of the priorities of the Global Organization of Parliamentarians Against Corruption (GOPAC) is to work towards an international convention or treaty against money laundering. The reason is this – the old adage 'a chain is as strong as its weakest link' certainly applies to money laundering activities. Criminals or corrupt leaders will always direct their money laundering efforts to those countries with the weakest legislative and regulatory environment. If all countries would make public international commitments to combat this scourge, the noose would be tightened further. This also includes the offshore banking centres and tax havens because although many of them have improved their efforts to combat money laundering, much more needs to be done. An international convention on money laundering must build on the Financial Action Task Force (FATF) standards, and not dilute them in any way. The notion of a convention should be abandoned if the negotiated result is a reduction in these internationally recognized standards.

3. Require the mandatory disclosure of income and assets of public officials.

Transparency is a very important tool in the fight against corruption and money laundering. While it might appear naïve to think that disclosure by public officials of their income and assets in some countries is an achievable goal, it is most worthy of pursuit. In most developed countries such mandatory disclosure requirements are commonplace. In Canada, we have an Ethics Commissioner who reports to Parliament and who sets out the public reporting requirements of Members of Parliament (with a similar system for Senators), Parliamentary Secretaries and Members of Cabinet. The Ethics Commissioner scrutinizes all the assets and liabilities of MP's and seeks redress if conflicts of interest occur (e.g. blind trusts for Parliamentary Secretaries and Ministers). Certain summary information is maintained on a publicly accessible web site for all to see (although some would argue the disclosure does not go far enough). This is the information that the Ethics Commissioner of the Parliament of Canada scrutinizes and provides summary information to the public about:

Public Declaration of Gifts, hospitality or other benefits received
Public Declaration of Liabilities
Public Declaration of Outside Activities
Public Declaration of Past Outside Activities
Public Declaration of Recusal
Summary Statement with Recusal
Summary Statement with Recusal & Part III
Summary Statement

4. Reward and support jurisdictions that practice good governance.

We need to reward good governance – countries like Ghana in Africa, which, under President John Kufuor's able leadership, has committed itself to fighting bribery and corruption. I had the great honour to meet President Kufuor when he came to Canada on a State Visit in 2001[109]. We met at Rideau Hall and discussed a range of topics including agricultural opportunities in the Afram Plains of Ghana – a very large and fertile area in that country. The President's desire was (and is!) to develop value-added and export opportunities in this area through public/private partnerships in an effort to promote economic development, and assist in the achievement of a sustainable national food supply for Ghana. We also discussed the availability of ferries that could serve on the huge Lake Volta in Ghana, a lake that extends into the vast interior of that country. Ferries were viewed, and perhaps still are, as a needed mode of transportation for people and goods to better connect the country. At that time I was aware of the 'bargain-basement' sale of three large ferries by the British Columbia Ferry Corporation, so I put my Ghanaian friends in touch with the company that was responsible for their disposal. The three ferries in question were eventually sold for a grand total of some $10 million, even though they had cost the B.C. taxpayer about $400 million! Unfortunately a transaction could not be consummated with the Ghanaian interests for a variety of reasons, including the need for major expensive retrofits to reduce the operating costs of the vessels, and the fact that the ships' draught exceeded the capacity of the lake in important locations. Finance was also a problem.

It was very frustrating to understand the many needs in a country like Ghana (one whose leader remains committed to good governance) and the inability to attract much needed foreign capital. The contrast on continents like Africa is always so startling. Compare Ghana with Zimbabwe, for example. In an August 30, 2002 letter I sent to then Prime Minister Jean Chrétien in August 2002 I referred to Zimbabwe as 'Land Reform Gone Terribly Wrong.'[110] I went on to say:

"The Government of Canada should be objecting in the strongest

---

[109] Speech on the Occasion of the Arrival to Canada of His Excellency John Agyekum Kufuor, President of the Republic of Ghana, and Her Excellency Theresa Kufuor, Governor General of Canada, Government of Canada, April 21 2004 < http://www.gg.ca/media/doc.asp?lang=e&DocID=1340>.

[110] Unpublished letter dated August 30 2002 from Roy Cullen, M.P. to Prime Minister Jean Chrétien.

terms possible to the undemocratic and tragically misguided methods of President Robert Mugabe. Appropriate international action should be implemented in concert with the United Nations and the road to sensible land reform begun."[111]

In this same letter I offered my views on Somalia:

"Given our unique relationship with Somalia, Canada should be playing a stronger leadership role in the search for governance models and development assistance that will lead to lasting peace, stability, and democracy in Somalia and the Horn of Africa. We should also support and assist the Somali-Canadian Diaspora in their efforts to bring about peace and security in the area."[112]

And on Ghana:

"As part of the plan for Africa that was agreed to at the recent G-8 meeting at Kananaskis, Canada should support countries like Ghana who, under the capable leadership of President Kufour, has made great strides in eliminating bribery and corruption. Last year I submitted two proposals to you on behalf of the Canada-Ghana Business Council – an organization that I helped to form. The first proposal seeks funding for a high-level Trade Mission from Ghana to Canada. The second initiative is the development of a *'Doing Business in Ghana'* guide, a publication that would assist Canadian businessmen and women in their business dealings in Ghana."

On April 26th 2003 I hosted, together with the Canadian International Development Agency (CIDA) and the Somali Press™, a Somalia Peace & Reconciliation conference in my riding of Etobicoke North in Toronto. About seventy-five members of the Somalia Diaspora in Toronto and elsewhere attended the conference and the group came up with thirteen recommendations. The conference's aims were to focus on two primary objectives, namely:

- What can Canada do, or should be doing, to assist in the reconstruction of Somalia? and,
- How can Canada provide leadership in the international community to achieve the objectives of re-construction and re-

---

[111] Ibid.
[112] Ibid.

development in Somalia?

The report contained thirteen different recommendations and concluded with the following statement:

"Canadians are an important resource for Canada and for the peace and reconciliation process in Somalia. As we wait for the results of the latest peace conference in Kenya, we must acknowledge that Canada could have a role in promoting peace and stability in the Horn of Africa. Canada's Somali-Canadian population would be willing to stand by the Canadian government's commitments to any involvement in the Somali peace and reconciliation process and indeed look towards Canada for a lead that could galvanize the inertia that characterizes the international community's position on Somalia."[113]

There is currently an interesting model in place, which rewards good governance; and that is the Millennium Challenge Corporation.

In January 2004, the US Congress passed a new compact for global development and created the Millennium Challenge Corporation (MCC) which links greater contributions from developed nations to greater responsibility from developing nations. The Millennium Challenge Account (MCA) is the vehicle through which development assistance is provided to those countries that rule justly, invest in their people, and encourage economic freedom. An initial $1 billion in funding was committed for fiscal year 2004, and President Bush has pledged to increase funding for the MCA to $5 billion a year starting in fiscal year 2006, roughly a 50% increase over then current US core development assistance.

"The MCA draws on lessons learned about development over the past 50 years:
- Aid is most effective when it reinforces sound political, economic and social policies - which are key to encouraging the inflows of private capital and increased trade - the real engines of economic growth;
- Development plans supported by a broad range of stakeholders, and for which countries have primary responsibility, engender

---
[113] Report on Somali Peace & Reconciliation Conference; April 26th 2003. Etobicoke North, Toronto, Canada.

country ownership and are more likely to succeed;
- Integrating monitoring and evaluation into the design of activities boosts effectiveness, accountability, and the transparency with which taxpayer resources are used." [114]

and is based on these key principles:
- Reduce Poverty through Economic Growth: The MCC will focus specifically on promoting sustainable economic growth that reduces poverty through investments in areas such as agriculture, education, private sector development, and capacity building.
- Reward Good Policy: Using objective indicators, countries will be selected to receive assistance based on their performance in governing justly, investing their citizens, and encouraging economic freedom.
- Operate in Partnership: Working closely with the MCC, countries that receive MCA assistance will be responsible for identifying the greatest barriers to their own development, ensuring civil society participation, and developing an MCA program. MCA participation will require a high-level commitment from the host government. Each MCA country will enter into a public Compact with the MCC that includes a multi-year plan for achieving shared development objectives and identifies the responsibilities of each partner in achieving those objectives.
- Focus on Results: MCA assistance will go to those countries that have developed well-designed programs with clear objectives, benchmarks to measure progress, procedures to ensure fiscal accountability for the use of MCA assistance, and a plan for effective monitoring and objective evaluation of results. Programs will be designed to enable progress to be sustained after the funding under the MCA Compact has ended." [115]

It has taken some time for the Millennium Challenge Corporation (MCC) to swing into action. In fact, the first grant under this program was only made on April 18 2005, over one year after the MCC's inception. The

---

[114] Millennium Challenge Corporation web page, Dec. 7 2004 (http://www.mca.gov/index.shtml).

[115] Ibid. (http://www.mca.gov/about_us/overview/index.shtml).

first approval was a grant of US$ 110 million to the Republic of Madagascar. Some are saying that the criteria that are used to access funding under the Millennium Challenge Account are too subjective. For example, a country cannot qualify for aid unless it ranks in the top half quartile of the least corrupt countries. Others argue that that the Millennium Challenge Corporation encourages countries to reform so that they can qualify for its funding. This debate has led for a call to review this initiative by the US Senate who began hearings on this topic in the spring of 2005.

5. Build capacity in developing countries so that they can help themselves.

As I indicated earlier, we can't solve all the challenges of the developing world without the active participation – financial and otherwise – of a country's citizens in their own economies. Wouldn't foreign investors, both public and private, considering Africa as an investment target like to witness Africans investing in Africa alongside their own capital? I would think so. I became aware of the critical importance of concepts like 'sweat equity' and local investor participation when I was exposed to the Northwest Territories Housing Corporation in Canada's north. Their fully subsidized properties were often in a state of poor repair, whereas the 'sweat equity' properties were well maintained. The lesson, in my judgment, is that you need local commitment, investment and participation for economic development initiatives to work effectively.

We also need to build capacity in developing countries in other areas – like an effective banking system, an independent and free media, as well as parliamentary accountability systems.

6. Encourage the formation of domestic savings and capital pools in developing countries.

In the short to medium term, given the generally bad state of governance and corruption, we need to be realistic about the appetite of the developed world to accelerate our aid to poorer countries. Taxpayers and voters in the developed world are not, and will not, support sixty to eighty cents of every aid dollar going to its intended purpose, with the balance lining the pockets of local officials and politicians and/or ending up in Swiss bank accounts. This scenario is simply not acceptable.

Investment capital will likewise not be incented to flow to the developing world. For example, while foreign direct investment (FDI) rose to a record US$644 billion worldwide in 1998, FDI to Africa declined from $9.4 billion in 1997 to $8.3 billion in 1998. Africa's share decreased from 2% to 1.3% of global FDI.[116]

So, what can be done? It begins, I believe, with the goal of increasing the levels of domestic savings in countries in the developing world. Some countries are rapidly moving in this direction as I learned at an Economic & Social Council meeting of the United Nations (ECOSOC) in Geneva in the year 2000 from the Minister of Finance and Economic Planning for Ghana. There is a wide range of public policies that encourage domestic savings – savings that can be invested in the developing economies.

As was noted in a February 2003 Canadian International Development Agency (C.I.D.A.) consultation document entitled Expanding Opportunities: Framework for Private Sector Development:

"Domestic savings, by far, represent the most important source of investible capital in all economies, typically accounting for well over 90 percent of finance on a net basis. Foreign savings, whether public (as in development assistance), or private (as in foreign direct investment and private capital flows), can be important and can catalyze change, but in the bigger picture, it remains a 'top-up', or complement, to domestic savings. While there are different behavioural attributes to different sizes of enterprises, in general, it is fair to say that the development of a vibrant, healthy and sufficiently diverse domestic private sector is generally seen as a precondition for attracting significant levels of foreign direct investment and integrating into the global economy."[117]

The UNDP report *Unleashing Entrepreneurship: Making Business Work for the Poor'* notes that "...domestic resources are much larger than actual or potential external resources. Domestic private investment averaged 10-12% of GDP in the 1990's, compared with 7% for domestic

---

[116] United Nations Economic Commission for Africa, *Transforming Africa's Economy: Economic Report on Africa 2000,* p.7.

[117] Canadian International Development Agency (C.I.D.A.) consultation document entitled Expanding Opportunities: Framework for Private Sector Development: February 2003.

public investment and 2-5% for foreign direct investment (FDI). Second, when informal resources are examined, such as potential land value, the domestic assets that can be tapped are much larger than cumulative FDI or private portfolio flows. Third, unleashing the domestic resources in an economy – both financial and entrepreneurial – is likely to create a more stable and sustainable pattern of growth."[118]

One huge source of funds for individuals in developing countries is remittances from relatives abroad. These entail regular payments sent by immigrants in Canada to their relatives in, say, India. "Most people remit just a few hundred dollars per transaction, but those contributions add up. Worldwide, remittances are now US$100 billion a year, according to the federal finance department. The largest recipient, Mexico, now receives more than US$16 billion a year in such transfers. India, the second highest, gets more than US$10 billion, a figure that appears to be growing... Jamaica, with a gross domestic product of just US$11.13 billion last year – received US$1.5 billion in remittances from around the world in 2002."[119]

To put these remittances into some context, the annual remittances from expatriates living in Canada to individuals in Jamaica is about equal to the annual development assistance funding flowing from the Canadian International Development Agency (CIDA) to Jamaica each year (just over $13 million)! These remittances are a form of development assistance and the funds are undoubtedly used primarily by the recipients for badly needed basic requirements like food, clothing, shelter and education – but imagine if this flow of capital, or some of it, could be used as a source of capital for starting or growing small businesses in these developing countries.

To accomplish this objective, however, investors must have confidence in the laws and regulatory environment in the country in which they are planning to invest. C.K. Prahalad refers to the need for *Transaction Governance Capacity (TGC)*[120]. By this he means the following:

"Fundamental to the evolution of capital markets and a vibrant

---

[118] *Unleashing Entrepreneurship: Making Business Work for the Poor*; UNDP, March 1 2004.

[119] *Toronto Star*, Sikander Hashmi, June 3, 2005, p. A-17.

[120] C.K. Prahalad, *The Fortune at the Bottom of the Pyramid*, (Wharton School Publishing, 2005), p. 81.

private sector is the need for a transparent market for capital, land, labour, commodities, and knowledge. Transparency results from widely understood and clearly enforced rules. Transactions involving these rules must be clear and unambiguous. Ownership and the transfer of ownership must be enforced...TGC is the capacity of a society to guarantee transparency in the process of economic transactions and the ability to enforce commercial contracts."[121]

Business does not have a big appetite for uncertainty. For investment to flow the rules of the game need to be clear, understood, reasonable and enforceable.

7. Expand micro credit – especially to women.

We should be focusing on micro finance by providing access to affordable credit for new and expanding small businesses in poor countries. When I had the opportunity to represent Canada's then Finance Paul Martin at meetings of the European Bank for Reconstruction & Development (EBRD) in 2001, the president of the EBRD at the time, Mr. Jean Lemierre, agreed with me that micro finance should be a priority - especially micro credit for women (not to be sexist, but women have a better track record with micro credit). The EBRD continues to promote and advance micro credit - advancing a small loan to a woman to buy a sewing machine or set of machines to start a small business, for example. I have seen the power of women and sewing machines in my own riding of Etobicoke North in Toronto. A group of Somali immigrant women some years ago established Haween Enterprises (Haween is derived from the Somali word for women) with an initial donation of a few Singer sewing machines. The company has grown substantially and now provides sewing, cutting and product development services for clothing and tote bags for schools, conferences and other institutions.

The payoffs from investments like this can be enormous. As the Oxfam Great Britain Policy Department noted in 1999:

"Increased household income is the single biggest factor in determining the rate of improvement in health and education status, pointing to the need for economic growth to be placed at the center of

---

[121] Ibid, p. 81.

poverty reduction policies."

One of the great micro credit success stories is the Grameen Bank in Bangladesh. In fact, the bank's founder, Muhammad Yunus, together with the Grameen Bank, were awarded the 2006 Nobel Peace Prize for their efforts to create economic and social development from below. This bank, which has grown from its start in 1976 to a portfolio of loans currently exceeding $1 billion to over 2 million borrowers, provides credit to the poorest of the poor in rural Bangladesh without the requirement for any collateral. It began by leasing underutilized fishing ponds and irrigation pumps and later expanded into venture capital and other businesses. Since the Grameen Bank (Grameen is the Bengali word for village) opened for business, 31 million people, ¾ of them women and ⅔ classified as the 'poorest of the poor' have received micro-loans in more than 40 countries, according to the *No-Nonsense Guide to International Development*. "It has financed businesses that manufacture everything from cosmetics and candles to bread, umbrellas, mosquito nets, even mobile phones. And what about the loan repayment rate? Ninety-eight percent, thanks in large part to the peer pressure that exists in villages to keep the community's reputation clean. That's a healthier way to channel tribal impulses than what most Muslim women are used to. Contrast that repayment rate to the ten percent recovery boasted by the Bangladesh Industrial Development Bank, which serves only people with property. No contest.[122]

The role of micro-credit for women also brings to light the question of gender in development and the conflict between the WID (Women in Development approach) versus the GAD (Gender in Development approach). There is a division among scholars as it applies to the question of gender in development politics.

The WID approach focuses more on the 'practical gender needs' of women, such as the basic need to adequate clean water, proper living conditions, employment, etc. Often international organizations like the World Bank have superficially tacked on these WID policies to development projects, without effective research and planning.[123] The GAD movement arose in 1986 by critiquing the WID approach as not sufficiently including

---

[122] Manji Irshad, *The Trouble with Islam*, (Random House Canada, 2003). p. 177.

[123] Tim Allen and Alan Thomas, (ed.), *Poverty and Development into the 21st Century*, (Oxford University Press, 2000). p. 388.

women in development planning. The GAD approach believes that in order to make effective changes for women in development, planning needs to include politically empowering women.[124] This approach focuses on the 'strategic gender needs' of women by creating a line of credit, abolishing domestic violence, eliminating inequalities in the division of labour (many countries in the developing world have legislation giving men a higher minimum wage then women), etc. The Grameen Bank is a good example of the GAD approach to women and development.

8. Unlock 'trapped' capital in developing countries.

In his book, *The Mystery of Capital*, Hernando de Soto explores why capitalism triumphs in the west and fails everywhere else. He is led to conclude that, far being a cultural phenomenon, much of the failure can be attributed to the lack of legal property systems in many developing countries. He estimates that "....the total value of the real estate held, but not legally owned by the poor of the Third World and former communist nations is at least US$9.3 trillion".[125] This is a staggering sum – nearly twice as much as the total value of all the companies listed on twenty of the world's main stock exchanges – including New York, Tokyo, London, Frankfurt, Toronto, Paris, Milan, the NASDAQ and a dozen others!

This represents 'dead capital'. For example, "In Haiti, ...68% of the city dwellers and 97% of people in the countryside living in housing to which nobody has clear legal title. In Egypt dead-capital housing is home for 92% of city dwellers and 83% of people in the countryside."[126]

Irshad Manji in her book *The Trouble with Islam*, describes 'dead capital' this way:

"Two examples of dead capital are black market businesses, which operate off the books and off the tax rolls, and properties claimed by squatters, who have no clear title to the parcels of land on which they live. In each case, we're talking about assets that poor people can't afford to register legally because it takes too much government paperwork, time, and fees. Lose the red tape, de Soto has shown, and the capital of the

---

[124] Ibid p. 388.
[125] Hernando de Soto, *The Mystery of Capital* (Black Swan Books, 2000). p.32.
[126] Ibid. p.30.

enterprising lower classes can explode into something truly constructive. Squatters can get collateral to secure mortgages and build less provisional lives. Cash-only businesses can expand into legal and value-added companies. Governments can thereby acquire taxable income. Everybody wins, particularly women and children. They're usually the ones who stay home in order to guard untitled land. Men, after all, must work. When property is documented, though, women can leave the premises to sell goods at the market, for instance, and children can go to school. After Peru implemented de Soto's ideas, school attendance rose by twenty-six percent..."[127]

What would the benefits be of 'freeing-up' this dead capital?

In his book, *The Fortune at the Bottom of the Pyramid*, C.K. Prahalad argues that "All forms of foreign investment in poor countries - whether aid, FDI by multinational firms (the private sector)) or philanthropy – are but a fraction of the potential for capital that is trapped in these countries."[128]

The political elites in developing countries are concluding that if they have to rely on sources of finance outside their respective countries, they will only 'muddle along' with no significant progress in uplifting their economies and the plight of their impoverished citizens.

9. Facilitate share ownership by employees.

We also need to encourage broad-based local ownership of companies in the developing world - through instruments like Employee Share Ownership Plans (ESOPs). In today's world, the flow of technology and information are just as important as the flow of goods and capital to developing economies. As Jeff Gates asserts in his book *The Ownership Solution*[129], "For development to take root and for prosperity to be enjoyed by more than a financially savvy few, the financial value of that development must not only be captured for those *residing* in the developing country; it must also be captured for a *broad base* of those residents (italics are the

---

[127] Manji, Irshad, *The Trouble with Islam* (Random House Canada, 2003). p. 179.

[128] C.K. Prahalad, *The Fortune at the Bottom of the Pyramid* (Wharton School Publishing, 2005). p. 79.

[129] Jeff Gates, *The Ownership Solution: Toward a Shared Capitalism for the 21st Century* (Addison-Wesley, 1998).

author's)".[130] Wages alone may not be enough, especially in an age where manufacturing flows to the lowest cost area.

Employee share ownership is driven by the notion that employees who have a stake in their company will be more motivated to enhance productivity because they will be able to share in the rewards. They are also better connected to the nation's economic system. These employees also achieve greater job satisfaction. Unlike stock option schemes, which are targeted at management, Employee Share Ownership Plans involve everyone in the firm – from the receptionist, to the inventory clerks, to the sales staff and senior management – it is an all-inclusive approach. Some years ago, a study was done of those companies listed on the Toronto Stock Exchange who were employee owned – and they exhibited a 34% enhancement in productivity and return on investment compared with companies with no such employee share participation.

Employee share purchase plans, while a step in the right direction, do not offer the advantages of ESOPs because participation is voluntary.

Gates argues that ownership-transforming financing techniques, like Employee Share Ownership Plans (ESOPs), will be necessary to accelerate growth in developing countries. Broad-based domestic ownership will assist in the development of the capital markets in those countries. The development of these markets will attract more outside investment as they acquire more liquidity and create exit strategy possibilities if required. Gates argues that development assistance tied to broad-based equity ownership would also address social justice concerns because of the greater inclusiveness of employee share ownership.

He argues, with merit, that we should be addressing root causes, not symptoms. Just as food is not the long-term solution to hunger, so is money not a cure for poverty. "A lack of money is a *symptom*, not a cause of poverty. Poverty is cured not with money but by gaining access to the productiveness – the skills and the tools – required to earn money."[131]

10. Stem the laundering of corrupt money.

Parliamentarians from around the world with whom I have spoken have

---
[130] Ibid, p. 231.
[131] Ibid, p. 33.

linked the need to fight corruption and money laundering simultaneously. Citizens and honest elected officials in corrupt countries are very dismayed when they witness the flight of corrupt funds, with impunity, to offshore banking centres in Switzerland, Luxembourg, the Bahamas and the like. Making it more difficult to launder corrupt money will act as a deterrent to corruption – even if the impact is not a huge one.

11. Build a stronger role for parliamentarians in demanding greater accountability and transparency from the executive branch of government.

Most parliaments have some type of separation of duties amongst the three main elements of governance – the executive branch, the legislative branch and the judiciary. One key role for the legislature is to hold the executive branch (those who have been charged with the responsibility to run the day-to-day operations of the government and to provide the government with overall policy direction) accountable to the citizenry. While corruption is certainly not limited to the executive branch in many countries, heads of state, ministers and other senior officials hold many of the levers of power and are most susceptible to bribes.

The legislature is able to, and should, put mechanisms in place to increase transparency and sanctions against corruption. This would include, but not be limited to, strong legislation making bribery and corruption illegal; an active, all-party and independent public accounts committee of the legislature which is charged with examining the revenue and expenses of the government to ensure probity and honesty in the conduct of the affairs of government; an Auditor General, or equivalent, who reports directly to parliament on the financial affairs of the government and issues an annual audit opinion on the government's financial statements.

12. Promote an independent judiciary, an independent Auditor General (or its equivalent), freedom of speech and freedom of the press, and an adequately resourced anti-corruption agency.

In some countries, it is well understood what the price is (from an unofficial tariff list) for a judge to bring in a not guilty verdict for someone charged with an offence. Kenya is a good example of this. Without an independent judiciary that is committed to the fight against corruption there is little hope to stem the tide of bribery and corruption because corrupt officials must, from time-to-time, be brought to justice to 'face the music'. With a corrupt judiciary, what are the chances of this happening? Besides, the judiciary set a very important example for society. If the judiciary is corrupt, what signal does that send? It reinforces the fact that bribery and corruption is an acceptable societal norm.

Freedom of speech and freedom of the press are also critically important ingredients in the fight against corruption, so that corrupt activities can be exposed to the public. In countries like Zimbabwe it is difficult, if not impossible, for this to happen because of the strict controls on the press and freedom of expression generally. In countries like Russia, after decades of state-controlled newspapers like Pravda and Isvestia, Russians are sceptical of the objectivity of the media, even though direct state control of the media has been relaxed. In Canada, the role of the media in exposing government mismanagement and corruption are legendary. While difficult and challenging for the government in power, the freedom of the press and freedom of expression keep a check on the level of corruption. The media plays a key role in forcing transparency and accountability. Institutions like Canada's Auditor General which reports directly to Parliament and whose mission is to hold the government to account for the way it spends money and manages the affairs of state is another important building block to greater transparency and accountability.

Some countries, like Russia, have formed anti-corruption agencies or commissions. This is to be encouraged notwithstanding the limited success of organizations like this. Anything that shines more light on this problem is a positive step.

13. Help the media to focus attention on corruption.

The media can play an important role in exposing corrupt activities. To do so, the public needs to have confidence in the objectivity of the media and confidence that the reporting is not driven by partisan interests. Whistle-blower legislation can be a useful tool to encourage and protect officials in the government who are witnessing inappropriate behaviour in government and who report to the media. Freedom of expression and the press (in Canada this is guaranteed by the Canadian Charter of Rights and Freedoms) is a necessary requisite to this, as is a public that has a low tolerance for bribery and corruption. Sometimes the stories need to be 'juicy' to get the media interested. But over time, if the reports are credible, the public's attention will be more easily focused on this type of activity.

14. Encourage the involvement of the private sector in development initiatives, including public/private partnerships.

The Commission on the Private Sector and Development, an initiative launched by the United Nations Development Program, was a high-level commission that was convened to provide analysis and evaluation of the key factors that are inhibiting the role of the private sector in development; to develop strategic recommendations on how to promote strong indigenous private sectors and initiate concrete programs with the highest potential impact in private sector development..

The Commission was asked two basic questions:
1) How can the potential of the private sector and entrepreneurship be unleashed in developing countries?; and,
2) How can the existing private sector be engaged in meeting that challenge?

In March 2004, the Commission released its report, *Unleashing Entrepreneurship: Making Business Work for the Poor.*

According to the Commission, the private sector can contribute to economic growth and empowering poor people by providing them with a greater array of cheaper goods and services. For the private sector to flourish, the following are needed, according to the Commission:
- Access to finance;
- Knowledge and skills; and,
- A level playing field for firms competing in the domestic market.

The Commission recommended actions in three spheres: in the public sphere, in the public-private sphere, and in the private sphere.

The Commission's recommendations are as follows:

Public Sphere

- *For governments in developing countries -*
  - reform regulations and strengthen the rule of law;
  - formalize the economy (e.g. property rights along the lines proposed by Hernando de Soto); and,
  - engage the private sector in the policy process.
- *For governments in developed countries –*
  - foster a conducive international macroeconomic environment and trade regime (e.g. access to international markets for exporters in developing countries);
  - redirect the operational strategies of multilateral and bilateral development institutions and agencies (e.g. better coordination); and,
  - untie aid (greater effectiveness and to stimulate local businesses in developing countries).
- *For multilateral development institutions –*
  - apply the Monterrey recommendation of specialization and partnership to private sector development activities (e.g. reduce or eliminate overlap); and,
  - address informality in developing countries (see above).

Public-private Sphere

- Facilitate access to broader financing actions;
- Assist skill and knowledge development; and
- Make possible sustainable delivery of basic services, particularly energy and water.

Public-private Sphere

- *For the private sector–*
  - channel private initiative into development efforts;
  - develop linkages with multinational and large domestic

companies to nurture smaller companies;
- pursue business opportunities in bottom-of-pyramid markets (i.e. the 4 billion people earning less than $1,500 per year); and,
- set standards (especially in corporate governance and transparency).
- *For civil society and labour organizations–*
- increase accountability in the system; and
- develop new partnerships and relationships to achieve common objectives.

The Commission's overall recommendations were forwarded for consideration to heads of the national and multilateral development agencies, as well as to leaders in the private sector.

The Co-chairs of this Commission were Right Hon. Paul Martin (Canada), Member of Parliament; Prime Minister of Canada, former Finance Minister, Canada; former owner Canada Steamship Lines, and Emesto Zedillo (Mexico). Director, Yale University, Centre for the Study of Globalization; former President, Mexico.

More recently, there has been more discussion about the importance of public-private partnerships in the context of international aid. There are a number of examples of successful public-private partnerships in the developing world. For example, the United Nations Development Program's (UNDP) Public-Private Partnerships for the Urban Environment (PPPUE) financial facility supports the development of innovative partnerships at the local level. These projects bring together financial resources and know-how into a risk sharing arrangement that allows projects to proceed, that perhaps otherwise wouldn't. One needs to be careful, however, about overstating the scope of Public-Private Partnerships (PPPs) and the role that they can play in developing countries. To engage the private sector, present and future earnings streams must, of necessity, be part of the equation. We tend to think of PPPs in the context of toll roads, for example, where there is a strong benefit/cost for users and the toll is affordable. They are particularly viable where no-cost alternatives exist in high-density traffic lanes.

But PPPs in the developing world have potential application in urban transit projects, and the development of an array of infrastructure. We should not believe, however, that the private sector would participate unless the financial returns are attractive and the risk levels acceptable.

While such evolution in thinking is positive, in my view we need a more fundamental re-think of international aid – one that is premised on the paramount importance of the development of financial markets in developing countries, and a greater amount of risk-taking and investment by local investors and entrepreneurs.

15. Pass effective laws that sanction individuals and corporations that pay bribes to public officials.

In some countries bribes can be deducted by corporations for income tax purposes as a legitimate business expense. Imagine what message this delivers to society! In some countries the sanctions for bribery and corruption by public officials are very light. One of the challenges is enacting legislation that introduces tougher sanctions for this type of behaviour when some or many of the legislators are corrupt themselves! This is what organizations like the Global Organization of Parliamentarians Against Corruption (GOPAC) is attempting to address by reaching parliamentarians around the world and building a critical mass of like-minded elected representatives who can force this type of legislation through their respective legislatures.

16. Reform the civil service in developing countries and reduce the 'culture of corruption' by paying public servants a fair wage and penalizing those who accept bribes.

If a bribe is required for service in a government department or agency, it is akin to a tax or user fee – with one big difference – the fee does not accrue to the general taxpayers, it goes directly into the pocket of the government employee! People are paying for the service either way, but a culture of bribery and corruption is being perpetuated. Wouldn't it be better to pay the public servants a decent wage and then credit any fees collected to the public purse? The economic cost is about the same, but one avoids perpetuating the notion that bribes are an acceptable societal norm.

For politicians in Mexico, when it comes to dealing with the drug lords, the choices are very clear – take the money and run and turn a blind eye – or have you and your family face the consequences of violence turned against you.

Many individuals with idealistic notions of fighting corruption get caught up in the endless cycle of corruption once they are elected. Many of them quickly forget the very reason they sought public office and reinforce the old adage –if you can't fight them, join them!

17. Reduce unnecessary red tape in governments to encourage entrepreneurship and reduce the temptation to expedite decisions through bribes.

One might intuitively think that large doses of government regulation are the perfect antidote for corruption. In fact, the evidence suggests that the exact opposite may be true. More 'red tape' can have the effect of creating a larger number of opportunities for would-be bribe givers to try and expedite the process with some cash. The World Bank's Cost of Doing Business Survey estimates that starting a business requires US$5,531 in Angola (more than eight times the per capita income) and about $28 in New Zealand (far less than 1% of the per capita income). This added 'red tape' increases the likelihood of corruption.

By the same token, too much discretion on the part of government bureaucrats can be viewed as a standing invitation for bribes to avoid unwanted obstacles being put in one's way. As Paul Salembier notes, "Even the best regulatory system cannot eliminate corruption. What it can do is avoid institutionalizing it. By maximizing predictability and minimizing the potential for corruption, a properly functioning regulatory system can be a key factor in maintaining investor confidence and ensuring economic vitality."[132]

18. Reduce the debt loads of poor countries that are committed to good governance and fighting corruption.

Countries like Nigeria are so mired in debt that it is next to impossible

---

[132] J. Paul Salembier, *Designing Regulatory Systems: A Template for Regulatory Rule-Making – PART I*; Statute Law Review, Volume 23, Number 3, p. 168.

for them to make the necessary changes to the way they operate because of the resources required just to service their national debt. The Heavily Indebted Poor Countries Initiative (HIPC) attempts to confront this problem by providing relief to those countries who are committed to good governance. The Government of Canada had played a leading role in this program and it should produce results. Good governance is the key, otherwise twenty years hence the global community will be faced again with the same problem as national assets and resources are siphoned off for the 'few.'

19. Remove trade barriers so that developing economies can more fully participate in the global economy.

Allowing developing countries the ability to grow their own economies is probably the factor most critical for success in the fight against corruption. A growing economy will help alleviate poverty and this, together with the right public institutions and public policies, should assist in the fight against corruption. Some of this is happening naturally as Thomas Friedman points out in his book, *The World is Flat: A Brief History of the 21st Century,* with developments like outsourcing and off shoring which are serving as a great boon to the economies of countries like India and China. We can do much more, however, so that countries like this and many others can market and sell their agricultural products and textiles into the developed world without running up against unfair tariff and non-tariff barriers. The WTO is addressing these matters but progress is painfully slow. As a show of good faith Canada will need to relax and eventually eliminate its own supply management regimes that artificially protect poultry and dairy farmers in Quebec and Ontario.

20. Better educate the public worldwide of the costs and negative impacts of bribery and corruption.

Too often bribery and corruption are seen as culturally acceptable norms that are engrained into society and difficult if not impossible to eliminate. It is true that eliminating bribery and corruption completely may be an impossible task, but we can surely do much better. The body politic needs to better understand the cost to society of bribery and corruption and also how it distorts the distribution of income and wealth. With the general public on side, politicians will be better armed for the fight.

CHAPTER 7

CONCLUSION

We know that poverty and corruption are linked. What we don't know for sure is which comes first – the poverty or the corruption. A reduction in the levels of bribery and corruption in any country will have a positive impact on the economy, which can reduce GDP anywhere from 8% to 15% – an enormous amount.

Some argue that corruption should not be a focal point in the fight against poverty in the less developed countries. Corruption, they point out, is endemic and woven into the socio-economic fabric of so many nations that we are wasting our time. This is a tempting notion that must be rejected for a number of reasons:
- Corruption is compounding the problem of poverty throughout the world because it inhibits public and private investment. Who wants to invest in countries where corruption creates additional uncertainty, as well as additional costs and the stigma of unethical conduct?
- Bribery and corruption lead to a sense of hopelessness amongst the citizenry and results in huge disparities in the distribution of national income and wealth. Few do well while many remain mired in poverty;
- Bribery and corruption provide fertile ground for international terrorists; and
- It is ethically and morally wrong to condone corruption;

While one cannot be naïve about these matters, even incremental progress in the fight against corruption at some point may be enough to turn the tide – probably never to the point when bribery and corruption are eliminated – but to a point when it is significantly reduced and no longer the accepted norm.

Organizations like the Global Organization of Parliamentarians against Corruption (GOPAC), with which I have been associated for a number of years, is having a positive impact by reaching out to like-minded parliamentarians around the world – those who have had enough of bribery and corruption and are prepared to do something about it.

It is in everyone's interest to try to lessen the gap between the rich and poor countries. Not only is it the right thing to do but attacking this problem is a real way will assist in creating more international stability and fewer opportunities for would-be terrorists. But reducing poverty is currently constrained by a number of factors – not the least of which is the proliferation of bribery and corruption in the developing world. It needs to be said that no country is immune from corruption. Transparency International offers the most objective ranking of countries around the world. Some are ranked as very corrupt (like Chad, Bangladesh, Turkmenistan, Burma and Haiti) and others are considered quite immune to corruption (Iceland, Finland, New Zealand, Denmark, and Singapore). Canada was in the top 5 of the least corrupt states until it encountered its own sponsorship scandal at which time it slid to 12th.

The fact that bribery and corruption of some sort exist in almost every country is no excuse for not dealing with this terrible problem. It is all a matter of degree. To compare the levels of bribery and corruption in Bangladesh with that in Iceland is almost laughable.

Money laundering goes hand-in-hand with corruption as well as with terrorism, drug crime and tax evasion. People in corrupt countries become disheartened when they witness corrupt money being laundered with ease by their leaders to offshore banking centers like Luxembourg and the Bahamas. More needs to be done on this front to remove some of the incentive to engage in corrupt activities. The ability to 'salt away' huge sums of money that rightly belongs to the average citizen is all too tempting for some.

We need to start thinking outside the box in our search for answers to the vexing challenges of bribery and corruption. The problem has too often been swept under the carpet in the past. Until James Wolfensohn took over the reins of the World Bank, it was politically incorrect to use terms like bribery and corruption. While this is no longer the case, terms like good governance are often used to avoid terms like corruption and bribery. Internationally, we have to accept that this is real problem and begin dealing with it more directly.

Continents like Africa, despite all the attention and promises does not seem to be making much headway in its fight against poverty. When trapped in endless circles of poverty, citizens seek their opportunities abroad – forcing unnatural migration patterns in these efforts to improve their standard of living. Most would rather stay at home, but they cannot if they want to improve their condition.

A crisis of confidence exists for both public and private investors who might otherwise be interested in supporting development projects, but who are also very concerned about the quality of governance in many of the less developed jurisdictions. Until such time as confidence is regained, the developing world will have to focus on ways to generate more capital domestically – whether through public policies that encourage more savings or more employee share ownership and micro credit, or through more developed local capital markets, or by freeing up 'unlocked capital' in real estate. Foreign investors, both public and private, will want to see the citizens of less developed countries invest in themselves. This will reduce risk, and over time reduce the extent of bribery and corruption.

At the same time, developing countries will need to more fully develop their institutions to support better governance. Institutions like a strong parliament, which can better hold their executive branch to account, together with a free press, a corrupt-free judiciary and Auditor General-like agencies. Better and more transparent reporting of the income and assets of public officials would be a good step forward as well. As well, reducing unneeded red tape helps to reduce the opportunities for bribery – as does paying bureaucrats a fair wage.

Internationally, the world community and organizations like the United Nations should consider naming corruption as a crime against humanity. Its impact on citizens can be almost as pernicious as genocide or ethnic cleansing. International conventions or treaties to stem the flow of laundered money would be another positive step recognizing that 'a chain is only as good as its weakest link.' We should also be removing artificial trade barriers which are preventing the less developed countries from reaching their full potential, which in turn would alleviate poverty in those countries. Again, on the international stage, more could be done to educate the citizens of the world about the cost and injustice of poverty and corruption.

Developed countries should have mechanisms by which to reward countries that enjoin the fight against corruption, with tangible support, so that the word starts to spread that if you reduce or eliminate corruption, the developed world will recognize this in a tangible way.

The task is a big one. Why would we avoid doing the right thing because the job is not easy? The costs, not just economic, of inaction are huge. We need to question how this problem has been addressed up until now and find new ways to attack it. We owe it to ourselves and to the generations that will follow us.

APPENDIX

THE INDEX OF PUBLIC GOVERNANCE

BY TONY HAHN

JUNE 2005

INTRODUCTION

The year 2005 has seen a number of significant developments around the issue of governance both in the developed and undeveloped world. Across the Atlantic, the recent rejection of the draft European Union constitution by the French and the Dutch were seen by many commentators as a rejection of economic integration and institutional overstretch in favour of the ethic of identity and national sovereignty. At home, there is much anxiety over the health of our democratic institutions, with political participation declining and public cynicism at an all-time high. Many activists are taking their causes outside of the political arena to raise awareness. Actor Liam Neeson tells us that in Africa, children are needlessly dying in the time it takes for Cameron Diaz and Justin Timberlake to snap their fingers, and furthermore, that "all these deaths are avoidable". For his part, Sir Bob Geldof is renewing his Live Aid project of 20 years ago to bring the issue of Third World poverty back to the public consciousness.

What is the informed observer to make of these issues of identity, sovereignty, and prosperity, and the role of government in reconciling all of the competing interests to create an environment where people are governed well? What is good governance, and how can it be measured?

This survey tries to answer that question. By taking four indices and combining them to make an overall ranking for 114 countries, policy analysts can gain a better understanding of how countries around the world are governing their citizens, and if those approaches are effective in creating opportunity, reducing poverty, and giving individuals around the globe a reason to believe in political engagement through liberal, democratic, free-market government as a worthwhile pursuit once again to improve quality of life for the human race.

Methodology

The Index of Public Governance combines four indices to come up with a composite ranking of 114 countries for which data exists.

The first two indices used are from the well-respected and non-partisan organization Freedom House and their indices of political rights and civil liberties as contained in the Freedom in the World 2004[133] report. Both of these indices rank countries from 1 (free) to 7 (not free) on both of these measures. Those scales have been changed to a scale of 2.5 (free) down to 0 (not free) by multiplying the original ranking by a factor of 1.666 for a score out of 10, and then dividing that figure by 4 to achieve a score out of 2.5.

The second index comes from Transparency International's Corruptions Perceptions Index 2004[134], which aims to measure public sector corruption. Rankings were originally out of 10, with a higher ranking indicating less corruption. These were then proportionally brought down to a rating out of 2.5 as well, in this case by dividing the original rating by a factor of 4, with a score of 2.5 being the highest possible score and 0 being the lowest possible score.

Finally, the last index comes from the Economic Freedom of the World 2004 Annual Report[135]. This index measures 38 variables across five themes: the size of government, legal structure and protection of property rights, access to sound money, international trade, and regulation. Once again, countries were ranked out of 10, with a higher ranking indicating more economic freedom. For the Index of Public Governance, these rankings were brought down to a score ranging from 0 to 2.5 by dividing the original ranking by 4, with 2.5 once again representing a perfect score.

The rankings out of 2.5 for each of the measures of political rights,

---

[133] Taken from Freedom House's *Freedom in the World 2004*, located at http://www.freedomhouse.org/research/freeworld/2004/table2004.pdf.

[134] Taken from Transparency International's *2004 Corruption Perceptions Index*, located at http://www.transparency.org/cpi/2004/cpi2004.en.html#cpi2004.

[135] Taken from the Economic Freedom Network's *2004 Annual Report*, located at http://www.freetheworld.com/2004/efw2004complete.pdf.

civil liberties, corruption and economic freedom were then added up for each country for a composite ranking out of 10.

This survey comes from a liberal, democratic, capitalist perspective. Rather than rehash the debate over the merits of big vs. small government, participatory democracy vs. rule by elites, it is recognized from the outset that ethical governments, voted in by their citizens while encouraging free enterprise and the exercise of civil liberties, are governments who provide the optimal conditions for the alleviation of poverty, the improvement of quality of life, and the creation and perpetuation of a robust, vibrant civic culture.

So how do the countries in the survey measure up?

Rankings

Corruption and Economic Freedom the Difference in the Liberal Democracies

New Zealand has the strongest model of public governance of all of the 110 countries surveyed. With a ranking of 9.45, it scores very well on all four measures.

Next in line are the four countries of Finland, Switzerland, Iceland and Denmark, with rankings of 9.35, 9.325, 9.275, and 9.275, respectively. In the case of Finland, Iceland and Denmark, their strengths were in the areas of corruption while Switzerland was one of only 5 countries to score over 8.0 on the Economic Freedom index, the others being front-runner New Zealand, the UK, the US and Singapore.

Rounding out the top ten are the United Kingdom (9.2), Australia (9.175), Sweden (9.125), Canada and the Netherlands (9.1), Luxembourg (9.05) and Austria and Norway (8.975). Each of these countries had a perfect score in the areas of political rights and civil liberties.

Interestingly, spots 11 and 12 belong to the United States and Germany, two countries who seem to be of increasingly divergent opinions on numerous issues. Their scores on economic freedom and corruption to mirror each other, with Germany getting 8.2 on corruption to the United States' 7.5, and the US getting 8.2 on economic freedom compared to Germany's 7.3. Celtic tiger Ireland is close behind at 13th, with room for improvement on corruption (7.5) and economic freedom (7.8). It will be interesting to see if further liberalization in Ireland has a positive effect on their Index rating in future years.

Japan and Italy: More Work to Do

One of the more surprising findings of the Index of Public Governance is that Japan (ranked 22nd with 8.075) and Italy (ranked 26th at 7.95) are outranked by Chile (15th at 8.675) and Uruguay (19th at 8.25).

While Italy scored perfectly on the political rights and civil liberties scales and received a 7.0 rating for economic freedom, it scored a dismal 4.8 on the corruption scale. Japan scored the same as Italy did (7.0) for economic freedom and had a 6.5 corruption rating, but lost points for civil liberties (2.1 – this is the only G-7 country with less than perfect ratings in both of the Freedom House rankings.)

Italy finds itself behind other rapidly transitioning Eastern European nations Slovenia (23rd, 8.05) and Estonia (24th, 8.01) as well. If these trends continue, Italy is in danger of remaining the sick man of Europe for some time to come, especially in the face of European enlargement.

Botswana Leads the Way – Or Does It?

In 29th place is the former British protectorate of Botswana, with a composite score of 7.52. Botswana is the leading African country, with Mauritius and South Africa close behind in 32nd place at 7.41.

However, it is estimated that over a third of Botswanans are living with HIV/AIDS, and unemployment is at over 20%.

The fact that a country like Botswana, which is facing considerable public health and public finance challenges, can finish on top of all African nations in the Index of Public Governance is reason to compare Index rankings with common indicators of development such as life expectancy, literacy and GDP per capita to see if the governance model is having a positive effect in the developing world.[136]

Comparing the life expectancies of Botswana, South Africa and Mauritius shows wide disparity. In Botswana, life expectancy is a measly

---

[136] All figures for life expectancy, literacy and GDP per capita are taken from the 2005 edition of the Central Intelligence Agency's *World Factbook* (http://www.odci.gov/cia/publications/factbook).

33.87, and in South Africa, figures are slightly better at 43.27. Mauritians can expect to live to 72.38 years of age.

Figures for GDP per capita and literacy, two common indicators of development, are comparable, but Botswana once again finishes at the bottom of all three measures. Botswana has GDP per capita of $9,200, South Africa's is at $11,100, and Mauritius is at $12,800. Mauritius also leads the way in literacy rates – 85.6% compared to S. Africa's 86.4% and Botswana's 79.8%.

Moving on down the list, the African country of Ghana places 43rd, at 6.675, ahead of transitioning, democratizing nations such as Romania and Argentina (tied for 52nd at 6.245). Ghana's life expectancy is 56 years of age, while Romanians can expect to live to 71.35 and Argentineans 75.91. Moreover, Ghana's literacy rate is at 74.8%, while 98.4% of Romanians and 97.1% of Argentineans can read – a difference of well over 20%.

Even on the measure of GDP per capita, Argentineans ($12,400) score much higher than both Romanians ($7,700) and Ghanaians ($2,300).

Let's compare two other countries, India and Turkey. On the Index of Public Governance, India scored 6.028 (57th place) and Turkey 5.094 (68th place).

Life expectancy in the two countries is significantly different, with Turkey at 72.36 years and India at 64.35 years. A total of 86.5% of Turks are literate, compared to a dismal 59.5% of East Indians. And in terms of GDP per capita, Turkey once again leads – $7,400, compared to India's $3,100.

Tied for 82nd place are two countries that could not be more different – Ukraine and Niger, with a rating of 4.377. Indicators show, however, that despite their identical ranking, life expectancy in the Ukraine is higher at 66.85 versus Niger's 42.13 years, with similar disparities in GDP per capita (Ukraine's $6,300 versus Niger's $900) and literacy (Ukraine's 99.7% versus Niger's 17.6%).

Finally, one other comparison is worth noting. War-torn Sierra Leone scores 4.844 (74th place) on the Index of Public Governance, ahead of both Russia (3.618, 91st place) and China (2.692, 99th place).

However, on all three indicators of development, there is no comparison.

Russia has a GDP per capita of $9,800, with China at $5,600 and Sierra Leone at $600. On literacy, 99.6% of Russians are literate, 90.9% of Chinese citizens are literate, but less than a third (31.4%) of those in Sierra Leone are literate. And finally, in terms of life expectancy, the Chinese live until 72.27 years of age on average, Russians 67.1 years of age, and those from Sierra Leone only 42.52 years of age.

These figures should give the reader pause, and they raise two important questions. First, what are the possible explanations for a generally positive ranking in the Index of Public Governance yet poor outcomes in key indicator areas such as life expectancy, literacy and GDP per capita? Secondly, how can two nations with identical rankings in the Index of Public Governance have wide disparities in terms of development indicators? Thirdly, and most importantly, are democratic institutions, free markets, and relatively uncorrupted governments enough to ensure quality of life?

Conclusions

Not only do we see differences at the middle and bottom of the Index of Public Governance in key indicator areas, but there are also significant differences at the top, too. For instance, #1-ranked New Zealand (9.45) has a GDP per capita of $23,200, while #16-ranked France (8.475) has a GDP per capita of $28,700. These differences, and those in the other key indicator areas as demonstrated above, indicate that there needs to be further research done over time to investigate what the effects of liberal, democratic, market-based reforms are. If the premise of this study is correct, countries like New Zealand will eventually eclipse France, but this of course depends on the political will to maintain good governance regimes.

Another conclusion can be drawn in terms of culture. For instance, what are the factors that have given rise to low life expectancy rates in Botswana, despite its structure of good governance? The rate of AIDS in Botswana has a very pronounced downward effect on the key indicator of life expectancy there. Over time, we will see if a country like Ghana, with much lower levels of infection, becomes more developed by comparison if it maintains and improves its governance model while resisting the conditions that lead to widespread sexually transmitted diseases. Conversely, a country like Botswana may decline in terms of life expectancy despite having all the right conditions for good governance. If that were to be the case, cultural differences could explain the variance.

One must also assign a role for history in the development of nations. Ukraine was part of the Soviet Empire for almost 80 years, which, despite all of its shortcomings, did lead to at least some industrialization as well as natural resource development. Niger, on the other hand, has had to deal with numerous coups since establishing free elections in 1995, and has never really had an adequate state apparatus to help promote economic development, or education and good health practices, for that matter. With the recent election of Viktor Yushchenko in the Ukraine and the continuing movement towards real democracy in Ukraine, these disparities will most likely increase.

Finally, another hard question must be asked; that is, what is the response of capital to governance regimes? In other words, do capital flows really respond to considerations of public sector corruption, political rights and civil liberties in addition to deregulation, ease of trade and the size of government overall? All indications from this snapshot are that capital goes where it can most easily make a return without regard for liberal, democratic norms.

However, it is important to look at this over time.[137]

Looking at an earlier example, although Russia has much higher GDP per capita than does Sierra Leone right now, if Sierra Leone sticks to its path of (comparatively) good governance, and Russia does not, then in proportional terms, that indicator of development should rise quite considerably in Sierra Leone *proportionately* in comparison with Russia - if there is truth in the argument that free markets, democratic institutions and uncorrupted governments lead to prosperity.

In another example, although India is well behind Turkey on the development indicators, India leads Turkey in the Index of Public Governance. Economically and politically, India continues to make great strides. If these reforms continue, there is no reason to believe that they will not narrow the gap between themselves and countries such as Turkey

---

[137] Due to incomplete data for one or more of the sub-indices in the Index of Public Governance, it is not possible to create an Index for previous years and compare it with outcomes now.

because of they are improving on their governance model.

On the other hand, if the standard of living, literacy and health outcomes improve in countries with weak models of governance, especially in comparison with countries with strong models of governance, further investigation will be required. It could very well be that the existence of one or more of the factors of either political rights, civil liberties, lack of corruption, and/or economic freedom do not have a positive effect one way or the other on the prosperity of a nation and its citizens.

It will be revealing to see how the countries in the Index fare five to ten years into the future.

My expectation and my hope is that despite the barriers posed by cultural and historical factors, as well as the seemingly lukewarm response of capital to political reforms, that countries such as Botswana, India and Sierra Leone will be examples for countries all across the developed and developing world – that liberal, capitalist democracy is indeed a force for good.

Tony Hahn – June 2005

Overall Rankings Plac		Political Rights	Civil Liberties	Corruption	Econ. Freedom
1. New Zealand	9.45	1/7 = 2.5	1/7 = 2.5	9.6/10 = 2.4	8.2/10 = 2.05
2. Finland	9.35	1/7 = 2.5	1/7 = 2.5	9.7/10 = 2.425	7.7/10 = 1.925
3. Switzerland	9.325	1/7 = 2.5	1/7 = 2.5	9.1/10 = 2.275	8.2/10 = 2.05
4. Iceland	9.275	1/7 = 2.5	1/7 = 2.5	9.5/10 = 2.375	7.6/10 = 1.9
Denmark	9.275	1/7 = 2.5	1/7 = 2.5	9.5/10 = 2.375	7.6/10 = 1.9
5. United Kingdom	9.2	1/7 = 2.5	1/7 = 2.5	8.6/10 = 2.15	8.2/10 = 1.875
6. Australia	9.175	1/7 = 2.5	1/7 = 2.5	8.8/10 = 2.2	7.9/10 = 1.975
7. Sweden	9.125	1/7 = 2.5	1/7 = 2.5	9.2/10 = 2.3	7.3/10 = 1.825
8. Netherlands	9.1	1/7 = 2.5	1/7 = 2.5	8.7/10 = 2.175	7.7/10 = 1.925
Canada	9.1	1/7 = 2.5	1/7 = 2.5	8.5/10 = 2.125	7.9/10 = 1.975
9. Luxembourg	9.05	1/7 = 2.5	1/7 = 2.5	8.4/10 = 2.1	7.8/10 = 1.95
10. Norway	8.975	1/7 = 2.5	1/7 = 2.5	8.9/10 = 2.225	7.0/10 = 1.75
Austria	8.975	1/7 = 2.5	1/7 = 2.5	8.4/10 = 2.1	7.5/10 = 1.875
11. U.S.A.	8.925	1/7 = 2.5	1/7 = 2.5	7.5/10 = 1.875	8.2/10 = 1.875
12. Germany	8.875	1/7 = 2.5	1/7 = 2.5	8.2/10 = 2.05	7.3/10 = 1.825
13. Ireland	8.825	1/7 = 2.5	1/7 = 2.5	7.5/10 = 1.875	7.8/10 = 1.95
14. Belgium	8.725	1/7 = 2.5	1/7 = 2.5	7.5/10 = 1.875	7.4/10 = 1.85

APPENDIX: THE INDEX OF PUBLIC GOVERNANCE   181

15. Chile	8.675	1/7 = 2.5	1/7 = 2.5	7.4/10 = 1.85	7.3/10 = 1.825
16. France	8.475	1/7 = 2.5	1/7 = 2.5	7.1/10 = 1.775	6.8/10 = 1.7
17. Malta	8.4	1/7 = 2.5	1/7 = 2.5	6.8/10 = 1.7	6.8/10 = 1.7
18. Portugal	8.375	1/7 = 2.5	1/7 = 2.5	6.3/10 = 1.575	7.2/10 = 1.8
19. Uruguay	8.25	1/7 = 2.5	1/7 = 2.5	6.8/10 = 1.7	6.2/10 = 1.55
20. Barbados	8.225	1/7 = 2.5	1/7 = 2.5	7.3/10 = 1.825	5.6/10 = 1.4
21. Spain	8.135	1/7 = 2.085	1/7 = 2.5	7.1/10 = 1.775	7.1/10 = 1.775
22. Japan	8.06	1/7 = 2.5	2/7 = 2.085	6.5/10 = 1.725	7.0/10 = 1.75
23. Slovenia	8.05	1/7 = 2.5	1/7 = 2.5	6.0/10 = 1.5	6.2/10 = 1.55
24. Estonia	8.01	1/7 = 2.5	2/7 = 2.085	6.0/10 = 1.5	7.7/10 = 1.925
25. Cyprus	8.0	1/7 = 2.5	1/7 = 2.5	5.4/10 = 1.35	6.6/10 = 1.65
26. Italy	7.95	1/7 = 2.5	1/7 = 2.5	4.8/10 = 1.2	7.0/10 = 1.75
27. Hungary	7.61	1/7 = 2.5	2/7 = 2.085	4.8/10 = 1.2	7.3/10 = 1.825
28. Costa Rica	7.585	1/7 = 2.5	2/7 = 2.085	4.9/10 = 1.225	7.1/10 = 1.775
29. Botswana	7.52	2/7 = 2.085	2/7 = 2.085	6/10 = 1.5	7.4/10 = 1.85
30. Lithuania	7.435	1/7 = 2.5	2/7 = 2.085	4.6/10 = 1.15	6.8/10 = 1.7
31. Israel	7.418	1/7 = 2.5	3/7 = 1.668	6.4/10 = 1.6	6.6/10 = 1.65
32. Mauritius	7.41	1/7 = 2.5	2/7 = 2.085	4.1/10 = 1.025	7.2/10 = 1.8
South Africa	7.41	1/7 = 2.5	2/7 = 2.085	4.5/10 = 1.125	6.8/10 = 1.7

33. Taiwan	7.395	2/7 = 2.085	2/7 = 2.085	5.6/10 = 1.4	7.3/10 = 1.825
34. Greece	7.385	1/7 = 2.5	2/7 = 2.085	4.3/10 = 1.075	6.9/10 = 1.725
35. Czech Rep.	7.36	1/7 = 2.5	2/7 = 2.085	4.2/10 = 1.05	6.9/10 = 1.725
36. Latvia	7.335	1/7 = 2.5	2/7 = 2.085	4.0/10 = 1.0	7.0/10 = 1.75
37. Panama	7.31	1/7 = 2.5	2/7 = 2.085	3.7/10 = 0.925	7.2/10 = 1.8
38. Slovakia	7.235	1/7 = 2.5	2/7 = 2.085	4/10 = 1.0	6.6/10 = 1.65
39. Belize	7.11	1/7 = 2.5	2/7 = 2.085	3.8/10 = 0.95	6.3/10 = 1.575
Bulgaria	7.11	1/7 = 2.5	2/7 = 2.085	4.1/10 = 1.025	6.0/10 = 1.5
40. South Korea	7.07	2/7 = 2.085	2/7 = 2.085	4.5/10 = 1.125	7.1/10 = 1.775
41. Poland	7.06	1/7 = 2.5	2/7 = 2.085	3.5/10 = 0.875	6.4/10 = 1.6
42. Mexico	6.695	2/7 = 2.085	2/7 = 2.085	3.6/10 = 0.9	6.5/10 = 1.625
43. Ghana	6.645	2/7 = 2.085	2/7 = 2.085	3.6/10 = 0.9	6.3/10 = 1.575
44. El Salvador	6.603	2/7 = 2.085	3/7 = 1.668	4.2/10 = 1.05	7.2/10 = 1.8
45. Singapore	6.56	5/7 = 0.834	4/7 = 1.251	9.3/10 = 2.325	8.6/10 = 2.15
46. Croatia	6.495	2/7 = 2.085	2/7 = 2.085	3.4/10 = 0.85	5.9/10 = 1.475
47. Namibia	6.378	2/7 = 2.085	3/7 = 1.668	4.1/10 = 1.025	6.4/10 = 1.6
48. Mali	6.37	2/7 = 2.085	2/7 = 2.085	3.2/10 = 0.8	5.6/10 = 1.4
49. Peru	6.328	2/7 = 2.085	3/7 = 1.668	3.5/10 = 0.875	6.8/10 = 1.7
Thailand	6.328	2/7 = 2.085	3/7 = 1.668	3.6/10 = 0.9	6.7/10 = 1.675
50. Benin	6.32	2/7 = 2.085	2/7 = 2.085	3.2/10 = 0.8	5.4/10 = 1.35

APPENDIX: THE INDEX OF PUBLIC GOVERNANCE   183

51. Jamaica	6.303	2/7 = 2.085	3/7 = 1.668	3.3/10 = 0.825	6.9/10 = 1.725
52. Argentina	6.245	2/7 = 2.085	2/7 = 2.085	2.5/10 = 0.625	5.8/10 = 1.45
Romania	6.245	2/7 = 2.085	2/7 = 2.085	2.9/10 = 0.725	5.4/10 = 1.35
53. Trinidad & Tobago	6.161	3/7 = 1.668	3/7 = 1.668	4.2/10 = 1.05	7.1/10 = 1.775
54. Brazil	6.153	2/7 = 2.085	3/7 = 1.668	3.4/10 = 0.85	6.2/10 = 1.55
55. Dominican Rep	6.128	3/7 = 1.668	2/7 = 2.085	2.9/10 = 0.725	6.6/10 = 1.65
56. Philippines	6.053	2/7 = 2.085	3/7 = 1.668	2.6/10 = 0.65	6.6/10 = 1.65
57. India	6.028	2/7 = 2.085	3/7 = 1.668	2.8/10 = 0.7	6.3/10 = 1.575
58. Senegal	5.953	2/7 = 2.085	3/7 = 1.668	3.0/10 = 0.75	5.8/10 = 1.45
59. Sri Lanka	5.711	3/7 = 1.668	3/7 = 1.668	3.5/10 = 0.875	6.0/10 = 1.5
60. Nicaragua	5.611	3/7 = 1.668	3/7 = 1.668	2.7/10 = 0.675	6.4/10 = 1.6
61. Honduras	5.511	3/7 = 1.668	3/7 = 1.668	2.3/10 = 0.575	6.4/10 = 1.6
Bolivia	5.511	3/7 = 1.668	3/7 = 1.668	2.2/10 = 0.55	6.5/10 = 1.625
62. Madagascar	5.486	3/7 = 1.668	3/7 = 1.668	3.1/10 = 0.775	5.5/10 = 1.375
63. Kenya	5.461	3/7 = 1.668	3/7 = 1.668	2.1/10 = 0.525	6.4/10 = 1.6
64. Papua New Guinea	5.386	3/7 = 1.668	3/7 = 1.668	2.6/10 = 0.65	5.6/10 = 1.4
Albania	5.386	3/7 = 1.668	3/7 = 1.668	2.5/10 = 0.625	5.7/10 = 1.425
65. Paraguay	5.361	3/7 = 1.668	3/7 = 1.668	1.9/10 = 0.475	6.2/10 = 1.55
66. Ecuador	5.336	3/7 = 1.668	3/7 = 1.668	2.4/10 = 0.6	5.6/10 = 1.4
67. Tanzania	5.194	4/7 = 1.251	3/7 = 1.668	2.8/10 = 0.7	6.3/10 = 1.575

68. Turkey	5.094	3/7 = 1.668	4/7 = 1.251	3.2/10 = 0.8	5.5/10 = 1.375
69. Kuwait	5.085	4/7 = 1.251	5/7 = 0.834	4.6/10 = 1.15	7.4/10 = 1.85
70. Malawi	4.994	3/7 = 1.668	4/7 = 1.251	2.8/10 = 0.7	5.5/10 = 1.375
71. Malaysia	4.96	5/7 = 0.834	4/7 = 1.251	5.0/10 = 1.25	6.5/10 = 1.625
72. Bahrain	4.893	5/7 = 0.834	5/7 = 0.834	5.8/10 = 1.45	7.1/10 = 1.775
73. Indonesia	4.869	3/7 = 1.668	4/7 = 1.251	2.0/10 = 0.5	5.8/10 = 1.45
74. Sierra Leone	4.844	4/7 = 1.251	3/7 = 1.668	2.3/10 = 0.575	5.2/10 = 1.35
75. Zambia	4.802	4/7 = 1.251	4/7 = 1.251	6.6/10 = 1.65	2.6/10 = 0.65
76. Colombia	4.777	4/7 = 1.251	4/7 = 1.251	3.8/10 = 0.95	5.3/10 = 1.325
77. Jordan	4.743	5/7 = 0.834	5/7 = 0.834	5.3/10 = 1.325	7.0/10 = 1.75
78. Guatemala	4.652	4/7 = 1.251	4/7 = 1.251	2.2/10 = 0.55	6.4/10 = 1.6
79. Venezuela	4.644	3/7 = 1.668	4/7 = 1.251	4.6/10 = 1.15	2.3/10 = 0.575
80. Oman	4.626	6/7 = 0.417	5/7 = 0.834	6.1/10 = 1.525	7.4/10 = 1.85
81. Uganda	4.385	5/7 = 0.834	4/7 = 1.251	6.6/10 = 1.65	2.6/10 = 0.65
82. Niger	4.377	4/7 = 1.251	4/7 = 1.251	2.2/10 = 0.55	5.3/10 = 1.325
Ukraine	4.377	4/7 = 1.251	4/7 = 1.251	5.3/10 = 1.325	2.2/10 = 0.55
83. Bangladesh	4.352	4/7 = 1.251	4/7 = 1.251	1.5/10 = 0.375	5.9/10 = 1.475
84. Nigeria	4.327	4/7 = 1.251	4/7 = 1.251	1.6/10 = 0.4	5.7/10 = 1.425
85. United Arab Emirates	4.234	6/7 = 0.417	6/7 = 0.417	7.5/10 = 1.875	6.1/10 = 1.525
86. Gabon	4.185	5/7 = 0.834	4/7 = 1.251	3.3/10 = 0.825	5.1/10 = 1.275

87. Nepal	4.11	5/7 = 0.834	4/7 = 1.251	2.8/10 = 0.625	5.6/10 = 1.4
88. Tunisia	4.076	6/7 = 0.417	5/7 = 0.834	5/10 = 1.25	63/10 = 1.575
89. Morocco	3.943	5/7 = 0.834	5/7 = 0.834	3.2/10 = 0.8	5.9/10 = 1.475
90. Congo (Rep.)	3.885	5/7 = 0.834	4/7 = 1.251	2.3/10 = 0.575	4.9/10 = 1.225
91. Russia	3.618	5/7 = 0.834	5/7 = 0.834	2.8/10 = 0.7	5.0/10 = 1.25
92. Cote d'Ivoire	3.201	6/7 = 0.417	5/7 = 0.834	2/10 = 0.5	5.8/10 = 1.45
92. Pakistan	3.201	6/7 = 0.417	5/7 = 0.834	2.1/10 = 0.525	5.7/10 = 1.425
93. Egypt	3.184	6/7 = 0.417	6/7 = 0.417	3.2/10 = 0.8	6.2/10 = 1.55
94. Algeria	3.076	6/7 = 0.417	5/7 = 0.834	2.7/10 = 0.675	4.6/10 = 1.15
95. Iran	3.059	6/7 = 0.417	6/7 = 0.417	2.9/10 = 0.725	6.0/10 = 1.5
96. Chad	3.026	6/7 = 0.417	5/7 = 0.834	1.7/10 = 0.425	5.4/10 = 1.35
97. Cameroon	2.759	6/7 = 0.417	6/7 = 0.417	2.1/10 = 0.525	5.6/10 = 1.4
98. Haiti	2.709	6/7 = 0.417	6/7 = 0.417	1.5/10 = 0.375	6.0/10 = 1.5
99. China	2.692	7/7 = 0	6/7 = 0.417	3.4/10 = 0.85	5.7/10 = 1.425
100. Congo (Dem.)	2.434	6/7 = 0.417	6/7 = 0.417	2/10 = 0.5	4.4/10 = 1.1
101. Zimbabwe	2.259	6/7 = 0.417	6/7 = 0.417	3.4/10 = 0.85	2.3/10 = 0.575
102. Syria	2.2	7/7 = 0.00	7/7 = 0.00	3.4/10 = 0.85	5.4/10 = 1.35
103. Myanmar (Burma)	1.05	7/7 = 0.00	7/7 = 0.00	1.7/10 = .425	2.5/10 = 0.625

Data Tables (Alphabetically By Country)		Political Rights	Civil Liberties	Corruption	Econ. Freedom
Albania	5.386	3/7 = 1.668	3/7 = 1.668	2.5/10 = 0.625	5.7/10 = 1.425
Algeria	3.076	6/7 = 0.417	5/7 = 0.834	2.7/10 = 0.675	4.6/10 = 1.15
Argentina	6.245	2/7 = 2.085	2/7 = 2.085	2.5/10 = 0.625	5.8/10 = 1.45
Australia	9.175	1/7 = 2.5	1/7 = 2.5	8.8/10 = 2.2	7.9/10 = 1.975
Austria	8.975	1/7 = 2.5	1/7 = 2.5	8.4/10 = 2.1	7.5/10 = 1.875
Bahrain	4.893	5/7 = 0.834	5/7 = 0.834	5.8/10 = 1.45	7.1/10 = 1.775
Bangladesh	4.352	4/7 = 1.251	4/7 = 1.251	1.5/10 = 0.375	5.9/10 = 1.475
Barbados	8.225	1/7 = 2.5	1/7 = 2.5	7.3/10 = 1.825	5.6/10 = 1.4
Belgium	8.725	1/7 = 2.5	1/7 = 2.5	7.5/10 = 1.875	7.4/10 = 1.85
Belize	7.11	1/7 = 2.5	2/7 = 2.085	3.8/10 = 0.95	6.3/10 = 1.575
Benin	6.32	2/7 = 2.085	2/7 = 2.085	3.2/10 = 0.8	5.4/10 = 1.35
Bolivia	5.511	3/7 = 1.668	3/7 = 1.668	2.2/10 = 0.55	6.5/10 = 1.625
Botswana	7.52	2/7 = 2.085	2/7 = 2.085	6/10 = 1.5	7.4/10 = 1.85
Brazil	6.153	2/7 = 2.085	3/7 = 1.668	3.4/10 = 0.85	6.2/10 = 1.55
Bulgaria	7.11	1/7 = 2.5	2/7 = 2.085	4.1/10 = 1.025	6.0/10 = 1.5
Cameroon	2.759	6/7 = 0.417	6/7 = 0.417	2.1/10 = 0.525	5.6/10 = 1.4
Canada	9.1	1/7 = 2.5	1/7 = 2.5	8.5/10 = 2.125	7.9/10 = 1.975
Chad	3.026	6/7 = 0.417	5/7 = 0.834	1.7/10 = 0.425	5.4/10 = 1.35

Chile	8.675	1/7 = 2.5	1/7 = 2.5	7.4/10 = 1.85	7.3/10 = 1.825
China	2.692	7/7 = 0	6/7 = 0.417	3.4/10 = 0.85	5.7/10 = 1.425
Colombia	4.777	4/7 = 1.251	4/7 = 1.251	3.8/10 = 0.95	5.3/10 = 1.325
Congo (Dem.)	2.434	6/7 = 0.417	6/7 = 0.417	2/10 = 0.5	4.4/10 = 1.1
Congo (Rep.)	3.885	5/7 = 0.834	4/7 = 1.251	2.3/10 = 0.575	4.9/10 = 1.225
Costa Rica	7.585	1/7 = 2.5	2/7 = 2.085	4.9/10 = 1.225	7.1/10 = 1.775
Cote d'Ivoire	3.201	6/7 = 0.417	5/7 = 0.834	2/10 = 0.5	5.8/10 = 1.45
Croatia	6.495	2/7 = 2.085	2/7 = 2.085	3.4/10 = 0.85	5.9/10 = 1.475
Cyprus	8.0	1/7 = 2.5	1/7 = 2.5	5.4/10 = 1.35	6.6/10 = 1.65
Czech Rep.	7.36	1/7 = 2.5	2/7 = 2.085	4.2/10 = 1.05	6.9/10 = 1.725
Denmark	9.275	1/7 = 2.5	1/7 = 2.5	9.5/10 = 2.375	7.6/10 = 1.9
Dominican Rep	6.128	3/7 = 1.668	2/7 = 2.085	2.9/10 = 0.725	6.6/10 = 1.65
Ecuador	5.336	3/7 = 1.668	3/7 = 1.668	2.4/10 = 0.6	5.6/10 = 1.4
Egypt	3.184	6/7 = 0.417	6/7 = 0.417	3.2/10 = 0.8	6.2/10 = 1.55
El Salvador	6.603	2/7 = 2.085	3/7 = 1.668	4.2/10 = 1.05	7.2/10 = 1.8
Estonia	8.01	1/7 = 2.5	2/7 = 2.085	6/10 = 1.5	7.7/10 = 1.925
Finland	9.35	1/7 = 2.5	1/7 = 2.5	9.7/10 = 2.425	7.7/10 = 1.925
France	8.475	1/7 = 2.5	1/7 = 2.5	7.1/10 = 1.775	6.8/10 = 1.7
Gabon	4.185	5/7 = 0.834	4/7 = 1.251	3.3/10 = 0.825	5.1/10 = 1.275

Germany	8.875	1/7 = 2.5	1/7 = 2.5	8.2/10 = 2.05	7.3/10 = 1.825
Ghana	6.645	2/7 = 2.085	2/7 = 2.085	3.6/10 = 0.9	6.3/10 = 1.575
Greece	7.385	1/7 = 2.5	2/7 = 2.085	4.3/10 = 1.075	6.9/10 = 1.725
Guatemala	4.652	4/7 = 1.251	4/7 = 1.251	2.2/10 = 0.55	6.4/10 = 1.6

Data Tables (Alphabetically By Country), cont'd		*Political Rights*	**Civil Liberties**	**Corruption**	**Econ. Freedom**
Haiti	2.709	6/7 = 0.417	6/7 = 0.417	1.5/10 = 0.375	6.0/10 = 1.5
Honduras	5.511	3/7 = 1.668	3/7 = 1.668	2.3/10 = 0.575	6.4/10 = 1.6
Hungary	7.61	1/7 = 2.5	2/7 = 2.085	4.8/10 = 1.2	7.3/10 = 1.825
Iceland	9.275	1/7 = 2.5	1/7 = 2.5	9.5/10 = 2.375	7.6/10 = 1.9
India	6.028	2/7 = 2.085	3/7 = 1.668	2.8/10 = 0.7	6.3/10 = 1.575
Indonesia	4.869	3/7 = 1.668	4/7 = 1.251	2.0/10 = 0.5	5.8/10 = 1.45
Iran	3.059	6/7 = 0.417	6/7 = 0.417	2.9/10 = 0.725	6.0/10 = 1.5
Ireland	8.825	1/7 = 2.5	1/7 = 2.5	7.5/10 = 1.875	7.8/10 = 1.95
Israel	7.418	1/7 = 2.5	3/7 = 1.668	6.4/10 = 1.6	6.6/10 = 1.65
Italy	7.95	1/7 = 2.5	1/7 = 2.5	4.8/10 = 1.2	7.0/10 = 1.75
Jamaica	6.303	2/7 = 2.085	3/7 = 1.668	3.3/10 = 0.825	6.9/10 = 1.725
Japan	8.06	1/7 = 2.5	2/7 = 2.085	6.5/10 = 1.725	7.0/10 = 1.75
Jordan	4.743	5/7 = 0.834	5/7 = 0.834	5.3/10 = 1.325	7.0/10 = 1.75

Kenya	**5.461**	3/7 = 1.668	3/7 = 1.668	2.1/10 = 0.525	6.4/10 = 1.6
Kuwait	**5.085**	4/7 = 1.251	5/7 = 0.834	4.6/10 = 1.15	7.4/10 = 1.85
Latvia	**7.335**	1/7 = 2.5	2/7 = 2.085	4.0/10 = 1.0	7.0/10 = 1.75
Lithuania	**7.435**	1/7 = 2.5	2/7 = 2.085	4.6/10 = 1.15	6.8/10 = 1.7
Luxembourg	**9.05**	1/7 = 2.5	1/7 = 2.5	8.4/10 = 2.1	7.8/10 = 1.95
Madagascar	**5.486**	3/7 = 1.668	3/7 = 1.668	3.1/10 = 0.775	5.5/10 = 1.375
Malawi	**4.994**	3/7 = 1.668	4/7 = 1.251	2.8/10 = 0.7	5.5/10 = 1.375
Malaysia	**4.96**	5/7 = 0.834	4/7 = 1.251	5/10 = 1.25	6.5/10 = 1.625
Mali	**6.37**	2/7 = 2.085	2/7 = 2.085	3.2/10 = 0.8	5.6/10 = 1.4
Malta	**8.4**	1/7 = 2.5	1/7 = 2.5	6.8/10 = 1.7	6.8/10 = 1.7
Mauritius	**7.41**	1/7 = 2.5	2/7 = 2.085	4.1/10 = 1.025	7.2/10 = 1.8
Mexico	**6.695**	2/7 = 2.085	2/7 = 2.085	3.6/10 = 0.9	6.5/10 = 1.625
Morocco	**3.943**	5/7 = 0.834	5/7 = 0.834	3.2/10 = 0.8	5.9/10 = 1.475
Myanmar (Burma)	**1.05**	7/7 = 0.00	7/7 = 0.00	1.7/10 = .425	2.5/10 = 0.625
Namibia	**6.378**	2/7 = 2.085	3/7 = 1.668	4.1/10 = 1.025	6.4/10 = 1.6
Nepal	**4.11**	5/7 = 0.834	4/7 = 1.251	2.8/10 = 0.625	5.6/10 = 1.4
Netherlands	**9.1**	1/7 = 2.5	1/7 = 2.5	8.7/10 = 2.175	7.7/10 = 1.925
New Zealand	**9.45**	1/7 = 2.5	1/7 = 2.5	9.6/10 = 2.4	8.2/10 = 2.05
Nicaragua	**5.611**	3/7 = 1.668	3/7 = 1.668	2.7/10 = 0.675	6.4/10 = 1.6
Niger	**4.377**	4/7 = 1.251	4/7 = 1.251	2.2/10 = 0.55	5.3/10 = 1.325

Nigeria	4.327	4/7 = 1.251	4/7 = 1.251	1.6/10 = 0.4	5.7/10 = 1.425
Norway	8.975	1/7 = 2.5	1/7 = 2.5	8.9/10 = 2.225	7.0/10 = 1.75
Oman	4.626	6/7 = 0.417	5/7 = 0.834	6.1/10 = 1.525	7.4/10 = 1.85

Data Tables (Alphabetically By Country), cont'		*Political Rights*	**Civil Liberties**	**Corruption**	**Econ. Freedom**
Pakistan	3.201	6/7 = 0.417	5/7 = 0.834	2.1/10 = 0.525	5.7/10 = 1.425
Panama	7.31	1/7 = 2.5	2/7 = 2.085	3.7/10 = 0.925	7.2/10 = 1.8
Papua New Guinea	5.386	3/7 = 1.668	3/7 = 1.668	2.6/10 = 0.65	5.6/10 = 1.4
Paraguay	5.361	3/7 = 1.668	3/7 = 1.668	1.9/10 = 0.475	6.2/10 = 1.55
Peru	6.328	2/7 = 2.085	3/7 = 1.668	3.5/10 = 0.875	6.8/10 = 1.7
Philippines	6.053	2/7 = 2.085	3/7 = 1.668	2.6/10 = 0.65	6.6/10 = 1.65
Poland	7.06	1/7 = 2.5	2/7 = 2.085	3.5/10 = 0.875	6.4/10 = 1.6
Portugal	8.375	1/7 = 2.5	1/7 = 2.5	6.3/10 = 1.575	7.2/10 = 1.8
Romania	6.245	2/7 = 2.085	2/7 = 2.085	2.9/10 = 0.725	5.4/10 = 1.35
Russia	3.618	5/7 = 0.834	5/7 = 0.834	2.8/10 = 0.7	5.0/10 = 1.25
Senegal	5.953	2/7 = 2.085	3/7 = 1.668	3/10 = 0.75	5.8/10 = 1.45
Sierra Leone	4.844	4/7 = 1.251	3/7 = 1.668	2.3/10 = 0.575	5.2/10 = 1.35
Singapore	6.56	5/7 = 0.834	4/7 = 1.251	9.3/10 = 2.325	8.6/10 = 2.15
Slovakia	7.235	1/7 = 2.5	2/7 = 2.085	4/10 = 1.0	6.6/10 = 1.65

APPENDIX: THE INDEX OF PUBLIC GOVERNANCE   191

Slovenia	8.05	1/7 = 2.5	1/7 = 2.5	6.0/10 = 1.5	6.2/10 = 1.55
South Africa	7.41	1/7 = 2.5	2/7 = 2.085	4.5/10 = 1.125	6.8/10 = 1.7
South Korea	7.07	2/7 = 2.085	2/7 = 2.085	4.5/10 = 1.125	7.1/10 = 1.775
Spain	8.135	1/7 = 2.085	1/7 = 2.5	7.1/10 = 1.775	7.1/10 = 1.775
Sri Lanka	5.711	3/7 = 1.668	3/7 = 1.668	3.5/10 = 0.875	6.0/10 = 1.5
Sweden	9.125	1/7 = 2.5	1/7 = 2.5	9.2/10 = 2.3	7.3/10 = 1.825
Switzerland	9.325	1/7 = 2.5	1/7 = 2.5	9.1/10 = 2.275	8.2/10 = 2.05
Syria	2.2	7/7 = 0.00	7/7 = 0.00	3.4/10 = 0.85	5.4/10 = 1.35
Taiwan	7.395	2/7 = 2.085	2/7 = 2.085	5.6/10 = 1.4	7.3/10 = 1.825
Tanzania	5.194	4/7 = 1.251	3/7 = 1.668	2.8/10 = 0.7	6.3/10 = 1.575
Thailand	6.328	2/7 = 2.085	3/7 = 1.668	3.6/10 = 0.9	6.7/10 = 1.675
Trinidad & Tobago	6.161	3/7 = 1.668	3/7 = 1.668	4.2/10 = 1.05	7.1/10 = 1.775
Turkey	5.094	3/7 = 1.668	4/7 = 1.251	3.2/10 = 0.8	5.5/10 = 1.375
Tunisia	4.076	6/7 = 0.417	5/7 = 0.834	5/10 = 1.25	63/10 = 1.575
Uganda	4.385	5/7 = 0.834	4/7 = 1.251	6.6/10 = 1.65	2.6/10 = 0.65
Ukraine	4.377	4/7 = 1.251	4/7 = 1.251	5.3/10 = 1.325	2.2/10 = 0.55
United Arab Emirates	4.234	6/7 = 0.417	6/7 = 0.417	7.5/10 = 1.875	6.1/10 = 1.525
United Kingdom	9.2	1/7 = 2.5	1/7 = 2.5	8.2/10 = 2.05	8.6/10 = 2.15
U.S.A.	8.925	1/7 = 2.5	1/7 = 2.5	8.2/10 = 2.05	7.5/10 = 1.875
Uruguay	8.25	1/7 = 2.5	1/7 = 2.5	6.8/10 = 1.7	6.2/10 = 1.55

Venezuela	**4.644**	3/7 = 1.668	4/7 = 1.251	4.6/10 = 1.15	2.3/10 = 0.575
Zambia	**4.802**	4/7 = 1.251	4/7 = 1.251	6.6/10 = 1.65	2.6/10 = 0.65
Zimbabwe	**2.259**	6/7 = 0.417	6/7 = 0.417	3.4/10 = 0.85	2.3/10 = 0.575

ACKNOWLEDGEMENTS

Writing a book is challenging and daunting task – not made any easier when one is a sitting Member of Parliament! Without the support and encouragement of a number of people, this project would not have been possible.

I would like to thank my wife, Ethne, for her encouragement and support throughout the development of this book, and for her thoughtful advice and time-consuming editing. Candice Debi assisted with some very useful research and analysis, and I am indebted to her for this. Len Pizzi was very helpful with data entry and information processing. Tony Hahn was very cooperative by allowing me to access his work - *The Index of Public Governance* – which helped me examine factors other than corruption and their impact on governance. Meaghan Campbell has been very helpful to me in my continuing work on the fight against money laundering.

My Conservative colleague in the House of Commons, John Williams, was a founding member of the *Global Organization of Parliamentarians Against Corruption* and he has been its guiding force ever since. I thank him for the inspiration that led me to conclude that even though the fight against corruption is a formidable challenge, it is well worth the effort. We are beginning to see some positive results, but much more needs to be done.

David Cuddemi, Ryan Murphy, and Fran Watt have provided me with needed assistance in the form of advice and logistics – both essential requirements for bringing this project to fruition.

Finally, I thank the constituents of Etobicoke North in Toronto for the confidence they have placed in me over the years, and for the opportunity to engage in the fight against corruption and money laundering – an important initiative I believe, and one that I am deeply committed to.

ISBN 1425127754